W9-CBO-177

SONG OF THE CITY

To Inez + Mike....
all the best

SONG OF THE CITY

AN INTIMATE PORTRAIT OF THE AMERICAN URBAN LANDSCAPE

BY NATHANIEL R. POPKIN

four walls eight windows | new york/london

Copyright © 2002 Nathaniel R. Popkin

PUBLISHED IN THE UNITED STATES BY
Four Walls Eight Windows
39 West 14th Street
New York, NY 10011
http://www.4w8w.com

UK OFFICES:
Four Walls Eight Windows/Turnaround
Unit 3 Olympia Trading Estate
Coburg Road, Wood Green
London N22 6TZ

FIRST PRINTING JUNE 2002

All rights reserved. No part of this book may be reproduced, stored in a database or other retrieval system, or transmitted in any form, by any means, including mechanical, electronic, photocopying, recording, or otherwise, without the prior written permission of the publisher.

LIBRARY OF CONGRESS CATALOGING-IN-PUBLICATION DATA:
Popkin, Nathaniel
  Song of the city / by Nathaniel Popkin.
    p. cm.
  ISBN: 1-56858-203-X
      1. City and town life—United States. 2. City dwellers—United States.
3. Philadelphia (Pa.) I. Title.
HT123.P635 2002
307.76'0973—dc21   2001-58363

Printed in Canada
Interior design by Sara E. Stemen

10 9 8 7 6 5 4 3 2 1

For R and L

When evening came on we were tearing out of Gary and toward South Chicago, the fire and smudge mouth of the city gorping to us. As the flamy bay shivers for home-coming Neopolitans. You enter your native water like a fish. And there sits the great fish god or Dagon. You then bear your soul like a minnow before Dagon, in your familiar water.

—Saul Bellow, *The Adventures of Augie March*

TABLE OF CONTENTS

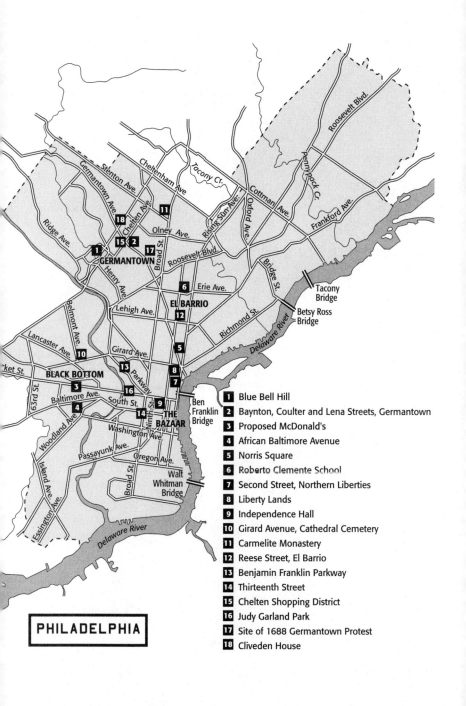

1 Blue Bell Hill
2 Baynton, Coulter and Lena Streets, Germantown
3 Proposed McDonald's
4 African Baltimore Avenue
5 Norris Square
6 Roberto Clemente School
7 Second Street, Northern Liberties
8 Liberty Lands
9 Independence Hall
10 Girard Avenue, Cathedral Cemetery
11 Carmelite Monastery
12 Reese Street, El Barrio
13 Benjamin Franklin Parkway
14 Thirteenth Street
15 Chelten Shopping District
16 Judy Garland Park
17 Site of 1688 Germantown Protest
18 Cliveden House

PHILADELPHIA

THE DAUGHTER
OF ZION

"**H**ow lonely sits the city that was full of people!" So begins the Lamentations, written by an unknown poet on the destruction of Jerusalem in 587 B.C. The Lamentations is the cry of an exiled people. It is their remembrance of a beautiful, perfect place and of pain, starvation, and abandonment. The Jews in King David's original city were walled in, trapped, then exiled by the Babylonians. The most fit were taken to serve in Babylon. Everyone else was either killed in battle or died of starvation. The city was left empty. It was looted and the temple destroyed.

In the eyes of the exiled and in the words of the poet, the abandoned city is like a person whose body is shattered and whose spirit is lonely. "How like a widow has she become, she that was great among the nations! She that was a princess among the cities has become a vassal. She weeps bitterly in the night, tears on her cheeks; among all her lovers she has none to comfort her; all her friends have dealt treacherously with her, they have become her enemies." I imagine that her tears flow in torrents through the abandoned streets of the city. They flow in remorse and self-hatred, as if the city were violated first and then destroyed. "All who honored her despise her, for they have seen her nakedness; yea, she herself groans, and turns her face away."

The face the Jews painted on the city was their own, or the face of the most beautiful woman among them. As she lay in disgrace, so did they, a people scorned by their own God and then besieged. "Our inheritance has been turned over to strangers, our homes to aliens." The aliens, in turn, left nothing but ashes. They destroyed everything but the idea of this perfect place.

3

But a city is its people. No level of abstraction can so easily erase human lives. Even in the Lamentations, which is an allegory for a morally lost and apparently sinful people, basic human stories shine through the text. Jerusalem in the sixth century B.C. is incomprehensible without understanding the lives of the Jews who had colonized it. From the poet of the Lamentations we learn of starving children fainting "in the streets of the city, as their life is poured out on their mothers' bosom." (We also learn of mothers eating their young.) We learn of princes stolen to Babylon, or worse. "Those who feasted on dainties perish in the streets; those who were brought up in purple lie on ash heaps." We meet a man who is driven into the darkness of exile, who is punished by God. In the terror and torment, we can sense love of Jerusalem and terrific lament.

Pity the poor exiled Jews who blew it, who lost their inheritance. Curse the Babylonians who razed Jerusalem. They destroyed "the joy of all the earth." Perhaps they did the Jews a favor by leveling the walls and the houses and the palace. Imagine the despair of the people if the Babylonians had left the city standing but empty and eerie. The Jews being led to exile would look back across the desert and see their city, appearing normal but actually barren of spirit and seed. The poet of the Lamentations understood that the Jews and their city were one. The city embodied them, and without them, it was ruined. The joy of all the earth was more than a heart-stopping site in the desert, more than a physical icon. Jerusalem was not exalted for its fine palace, but for the rapturous breath of its holy people.

There are scholars who measure cities not in personal moments but in economic movements, government institutions, and tax structures. To be sure, the ebb and flow of capital and people, power, taste, and values impacts every block in every city in the world, and every person living there. But gauging the bristly street and walking on cracked and deeply worn sidewalks forces us to realize that somewhere below economic and political mechanisms real people create, struggle, live, sleep, and fuck. They love. They misinterpret. They feel bitterness. In so doing, they alter their environment in meaningful and far-flung ways.

The city continues into time, not as an ordinary progression or a simple narrative. A city of human beings cannot be reduced to the booster's cry, to bulldozing forward. Human lives will not bend to a fable of growth and decline, rebirth, renaissance, or renewal. Once the place is settled (and even that event can never be assigned an exact moment), it moves forward, but only as the seasons change and the years pass by. Nothing else about the city is a linear progression. Think of the city as a collection of swarming cells that change, adapt, grow, shrink, and grow simultaneously. Imagine hundreds or thousands or millions of cells, each living and dying not in parallel or even in sequence, but overlapping from one generation to the next. The whole place moves in several directions at once. Unless calamity hits, no city dies in a single instant. Despite what you read in the papers, no city, no neighborhood even, is ever miraculously reborn. But people in the city die and others are born. In this simple process of human life, the city is reinterpreted and reshaped, without ever letting any of us go.

Once we learn to imagine the city as a being that can be seen, touched, smelled, and heard, we can sense the city. We sense its heart beating in the people who come and go, live and die. We sense the city chortling across time in the hands of those who inherit it, who claim it as their own. We sense its body changing as we walk through streets and neighborhoods. We sense its soul erupting in festival and ritual, in terror, and in loneliness. We sense it regenerating in the hands of those who build and rebuild, adapt and create.

The city in this book is Philadelphia, not Jerusalem. (Though I note a city called Philadelphia northeast of the Dead Sea on a biblical map from the first century, my city is in the most rural state in contemporary America, Pennsylvania.) And this is not a lament or a celebration, but a song of the city where I have lived on and off, but mostly on, for the past fourteen years. I wonder if the Lamentations were written about this Philadelphia, would the city be personified as a princess, a widow, or a defiled whore? Most would have to say Philadelphia is a sucker to big corporate interests and anyone who has a dream to sell, but I won't judge her like that. She is, in a way, human and like every one of us a princess, a widow, and a whore.

On these pages, I pull apart the city. I examine the nature of its *pulse*. The city's pulse is the energy we feel on the street, its life force. This force is really the human cycle of life and death. The pulse continues as long as these cycles last, as hundreds of thousands are born or die, as they come and go. The city's pulse is as much about death as it is about life. We can measure it in the waves of people handing the city down through time, in births and deaths inside the fortress wall, in immigrants and migrants, even the invaders and the exiled. What I find remarkable about this process is that at any given moment, a city is its people *and* all those who came before them. So Jerusalem is contested ground. Almost twenty-six centuries later the widow that was a princess, the *daughter of Zion*, is still there atop the mount. Just forty-eight years after the exile, the Jews came back and then Greeks and Romans, Christians and Muslims. Those who came by force, those who simply remembered her and returned became the blood in her veins. Always, throughout time, her heart keeps beating.

We notice the beating pulse on the street. The pulse is contained in people, in waves of faces, in bodies of old and young, as time pushes generations along. But the street itself, the *body* of the city, is a physical manifestation of its pulse. The city's body is its suburbs, neighborhoods, barrios, streets, corners, monuments, and buildings. From my window, I see the city's body. For more than three centuries, people have come and gone from this block. They have built and rebuilt. I see the back of a crumbling brick building, once and still the Second Ward Republican Club, inhabited by a handful of survivors from the Republican machine of the early twentieth century. Ailanthus trees grow shamelessly around the building. A Dr. Pepper sign of another era remains in the window. I see a mansion built a few years ago of cinder block and steel sandwiched between row houses covered in sloppy Roman-colored stucco. Above one, I see an elegant curved dormer window in need of paint and repair. I see a gated asphalt parking lot full of fancy cars. I see the city's body. It is mangled and torn. It is handsome and robust.

At night, despite the highway-style lights that glow in my window, it is hard to make out the buildings across the way. The details are lost; the street trees have no definition. They merely block the view. Now, sensing the city requires other faculties. At night, voices on the street sound louder. From my window, I hear feet. I hear hurried feet. I sense anticipation. I see wickedness and madness in the shadows, between the cars. I hear shouting and grunting. I sense the *soul* of the city.

The city's soul is the spirit of its people: neither good nor evil, neither shameful nor proud. The Lamentations is itself a struggle to understand the soul of ancient Jerusalem, the soul of a proud woman, too rebellious, too haughty, now deeply ashamed. The soul of this city is enveloped in the folds of its body. I find it in stories of passion and determination and foolery. It exists in memories, in sudden terror, and in mass celebration. We glimpse the soul of the city by listening to what people say to each other, by noticing the way they look at each other, and by hearing their shared silence.

The poet of the Lamentations probably believed that Jerusalem had been destroyed forever. He documents complete and graphic annihilation of the people of the city. He wonders if they have exceeded even God's limitless patience. Yet he prays that God will listen to the earnest pleas and restore the city. The poet sees the seeds of regeneration in God's ultimate compassion. Perhaps Jerusalem will be restored to them. The seed of Jerusalem in the sixth century B.C. was the idea of a people living in a perfect city under a single God. When the city was destroyed, the Jews cast the idea across the sand. The wind buried it there in the remains of the old temple until the Babylonians granted them freedom to return.

The city as a living being has the capacity to reproduce, really to recreate itself. Every person in the city buries seeds in the ground; in turn, *their* city grows around them. Outside my window, these seeds of change toss in the wind. When they fall and take root, the city changes, always becoming a new version of itself. By far the most powerful seeds are those cast by people together. Seeds cast with purpose and deeply planted affect the city's pulse, body, and its soul. In Philadelphia these days, neighbors working together cast the strongest seeds. No longer do the city's fathers pull real weight; government itself just nibbles around the edges, vision-less, contentedly building stadiums and museums. But neighbors, sometimes institutions and churches, groups of individuals, artists and the like, change the city. They cast seed in small plans, in literal toil, in hours spent tending flowers. The toil keeps the city alive.

"How lonely sits the city that was full of people!" That's just it: every city is lonely for people. No matter how many it has, it wants more. The city is insatiable. Yet we who observe the cityscape don't seem to accept this. We want to think of cities as buildings, statis-tics, and abstract concepts. We look at a city street and we see economic stratification or Disneyfication or gentrification or pre-servation or deindustrialization. We categorize and analyze. We try to understand trends in ten-year segments. We measure begin-nings and endings.

I think that as Americans we fear this sensual, human city. We fear each other and ourselves. We fear commitment. The Jews wanted nothing but to march back across the desert to Jerusalem and embrace their princess, their city. Personify a place and you might fall in love, you might never want to leave. No American wishes to be so content and held so still. So we head for the highway. We eat fast and move on. When we talk about cities, we rank them, we measure them, we compare costs, stadiums, square feet of commercial space. We rarely discuss human lives, suffering, love, or beauty. But that's what cities are for.

For several years, I have walked the streets of the city searching and listening. I left familiar places and kept walking. When I could walk no more, I took the subway, the bus, or the train. Philadelphia is a vast city of small streets. It is measured in rhythms of row houses and trees, enormous mostly vacant factories, giant schools and churches, mansions, bulky apartment buildings, and vacant lots. This landscape seems endless. At 135 square miles, to someone on foot, it *is* endless.

As I walked, I met people. I listened to their stories. The city in these pages is alive with these personal experiences. My city, the city we can imagine to have a pulse, a body, soul, and seed, is replete with people from every corner. Many of them shared with me their own personal stories and family histories. They described their relationships with the city. They related moments of violence, sadness, struggle, and light. Mostly I listened, scribbling. I followed them on walks through special places. You will find those places in the pages that follow. In the stories, you will discover not only the vastness of the city's landscape but also its people. My city is their stories. It is a powerful, reckless place. Let it shroud you with the crush of voices.

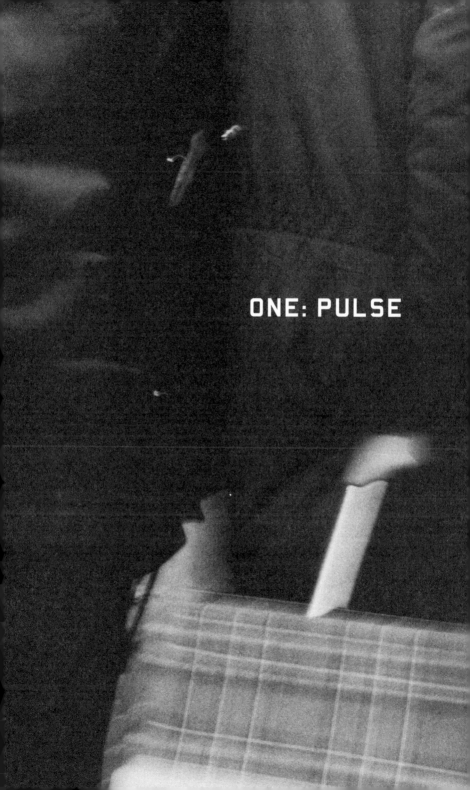

ONE: PULSE

I. WHAT THE CITY TEACHES US

O N the street we feel the city's pulse. This energy, constant
motion, really the interplay between life and death, old and
new, is what we value in cities. Cities exist in the tension, in historical references, in nostalgia and stories, in *moda* and old factories, in new buildings replacing old and others restored to some
particular moment, in a person dying and another being born. I
hold in my hand an old photograph of a city street. I can imagine
the sounds. I walk the same streets as Franklin, Capone, Whitman, and Baldwin. The city connects all of us here today to the
past. Seeing ourselves in the continuum, we connect ourselves to
the city. We are part of the rhythm.

In the forties and fifties, the *Life* photographer Andreas Feininger took a series of shots of New York. Feininger saw crammed
streets, the airy waterfront. His lenses bent the streetscape and he
took everything in. In one of his early photos, it appears to be dawn.
The sun is blasting over the East River. There's enough hard current
of pure sunlight to filter through the dense smoke and smog and
the gray industrial grit of Manhattan in 1942. This is a deeply evoca-
tive and beautiful portrait, the light glancing the buildings just
right, the steam caught still hovering above the apartments, factories, and skyscrapers. In the foreground along the Hudson River it is
dark still, the sun only managing to illuminate a dancing clothesline and the few cars parked near the piers.

What makes the photograph so engaging, so much more than
pure landscape, is the certain way that Feininger captures the
melancholy evidence of the human endeavor. The buildings of
Gotham dominate this photograph: they're so tall that a few stretch

beyond the frame of the picture. They are dark and elegant, classical, and foreboding. But after a while, I notice the substrata—a fading billboard for Lolwer's Brewery, the clothesline that does not seem to belong. I imagine that the cars must have pulled quickly up to the pier, doors slamming, the drivers escaping into the cold early morning air.

I flip forward one page in the book. Here is Fifth Avenue, midtown in 1950. The spring air is gray and smoggy. Fifth Avenue itself is gridlocked with buses and taxis. The zoom lens condensed five blocks into one view, but that only makes the point clearer. The street and sidewalk are madness. Every inch is filled. Office workers are out to lunch in their seersucker jackets, bow ties, and bowler hats. Taxis cross Fifth Avenue enveloped by people talking, walking, staring, squinting, posing, waddling, heaving, and strutting. The particular ozone-reflecting character of the sun at noon is like a stage light. But this is Fifth Avenue, not Broadway, and no one in particular has choreographed this dance. It's a mass solo.

*

In the last picture of this progression it is winter, but there is no snow on the ground. Barren trees—twisted, bent, open and bristly, naked to the eyes of New York—stand still. There are maybe thirty of them, but only four or five have thick, black trunks. The rest are saplings waiting for March to end. The sun is bright though the day is more than half over. The shadows are long. Telephone lines cross the bottom of the picture like trolley tracks suspended in midair.

This is a picture of a Jewish cemetery in Brooklyn. Thousands of gravestones of every shape and size stand erect and crammed together facing the low angling sun. Levy, Abelow, Solomon, Silverstein, Feder. Wolf, Weiss, Glass, Father, Dear Wife, Brother, hundreds of Mothers, Rest in Peace. These people are wedged and cramped in death as in tenement life. Of course this last picture of the Brooklyn cemetery is in its very essence about human life, community, the act of rubbing shoulders with others even in death. This is not an ornate cemetery. Few are bragging about material wealth collected in life as they rest in peace. None stand out, so that only the family ties, dependencies, and relationships seem to matter. The telephone lines take on meaning, evidence of man's vain endeavor in life. Here, Feininger captured life and death, both standing naked, tangible, both at once beautiful and mutinous and terrifyingly ordinary. His cemetery might well represent the city itself.

We are all part of the city's pulse. When we step onto a crowded avenue, a busy port or plaza, we say *what a vibrant place*. We sense the force of life, period. When we see a crowded street like Fifth Avenue in 1950, we are overwhelmed by its maddening living energy. A city creates this magnetic force, compelling us to rub and smell one another, taste, touch, and feel the tight, dynamic, and immediate physical world. On every corner and narrow subway platform and in every newsstand, on every scaffold and thickly packed bus we encounter equivocal faces, sad and easy and forthcoming faces. We are each in a singular instant of a singular life, but together, jumbled in that same instant. What we feel on the crowded bus is an immediate jolt. It is marvelous. So many living so closely—a human rush of voices and arms and leather soles all moving forward. Forward. This is the direction that moves us, that thrills us. In our eyes the city can be a progressive machine. It can represent life, life now and life ahead. We do not notice death. It is concealed.

Perhaps the equation is different in Philadelphia. Bones are scattered throughout the city and in some particular places so thickly that we sometimes have to pick through layers of detritus to feel the city's pulse. In the eighties, parts of Philadelphia shook

with crack fever. Hundreds were killed each year. Children played
on the stoop, one minute chasing each other or making circles with
tricycles, the next they were dead on the ground. Death in the city
is unavoidable. It is part of its foundation, as sensual and at times
as overbearing as the life all around, as familiar as the voices and
the chortle of the bus's diesel engine as it hauls dutiful workers
from houses to offices and back again.

When we imagine the city, we envision a process of life and
death. Once started, the process might never end. (The Babylonians razed Jerusalem 2,600 years ago and killed and exiled
the entire population, and still the city's heart kept beating
through successive waves of invasion and adaptation.) The ancient Jews called Jerusalem the Daughter of Zion. She was the
physical representation of the grace of their religion. They
adorned her with the jewels of their law. Her beauty was the purity of their actions. We can imagine the contemporary city,
with its palpable evidence of life and death, as a representation
of the earliest pagan religions, as a manifestation of the worship
of nature.

Like in the Brooklyn cemetery, life and death surround us.
They are inseparable, a single force. The city confronts us shamelessly with this evidence. This display is the city's greatest gift. It
is why in such a technical, sanitized nation, we need our cities. We
need them, as we need wilderness, to remind us of time and seasons, of hunger and viciousness. But the city's lesson is more direct than the countryside's. It is more obviously about human life,
about our own terrifying mortality, about our terrible ambition.
Consequently, the city is our finest teacher of the nature of
human beings. There is no protection from this lesson. Once we
understand it, we cease to fear the city. We become willing to embrace the forceful pulse and consume the street's energy. The energy nourishes us. It joins us to those around and to those who

came before us. We are joined as one story, connected as a single continuous human evolution writ across a street grid that once circumscribed a lowland field. Gaining a sense of our own origins, we see our lives in context.

2. FEELING THE PULSE

ON a dark and quiet morning, with slate air blanketing the city, I sat at my desk in the third floor of my house. The sky was thick and unforgiving, like the introspective mood of a film by the Russian director Sokurov, but denser and even flatter. This was the third day of rain and premature cold. The water blew in torrents, a sea wind, wet. It was August fourteenth. The rain had come in waves all night. I must not have realized when it let up because the voice from below startled me. It was forceful but smooth. Who would be on the street singing on a morning like this one?

I'm a born fool but what can I do?
Why was I born?
Why do I try to draw you in?
I'm a born fool but what can I do?
Why was I born to love you?

The voice was Sinatra's. Was he back for more in South Philly? Blinded by death, did he overshoot his old haunt, Palumbo's Nostalgia Room? Perhaps he went there first, found instead a Rite Aid pharmacy and stumbled to this corner. Had he forgotten about the fire on Ninth Street? The possibilities rolled through my imagination. Stranger things have happened in this neighborhood. And Frank is loved here. Storeowners on Ninth Street pipe his music to the sidewalk everyday. When he died, he was mourned like one of the neighborhood's own. I knew it wasn't Frank, but who had stolen his voice?

I went downstairs and outside. It was cooler out than inside. I followed the voice down the alley to the park. There *was* a crooner in the green park. Sitting alone on the rain-soaked wooden bench, he was drunk, his white beard matted. He wore a black baseball cap and had a shopping cart full of a homeless man's collected imagination. So this is the reincarnation of Sinatra? The man wheeled on his bench and bellowed. He waved his arms, made circles in the air. Only when I came within a few feet, did I hear him slur. A German shepherd barked, his snout low to the ground, inspiring the crooner.

How much is that doggie in the window?
The one with the waggly tail.
How much is that doggie in the window?
I wonder if he's for sale.

When he hit the next stanza, the rain that had taken a break came again, at first gently, then harder and steady. The rain was saturating and thick. Even the campy, drunk, dark-faced crooner noticed. He ended the show. Draped in a heavy black overcoat, he lifted his body, then bent over a trash can. I watched him sift through the soggy returns. Finding nothing but shit-filled plastic bags, he walked southwest out of the park. The rain engulfed his silent black figure. I went back inside. Upstairs, I still heard the crooner's voice, as if it were trapped in the sponge air. Now, in the air or in my mind, it was indistinguishable from Sinatra's. I was convinced. The dead never leave the city. And they never leave the living alone.

Or is it the other way around? If we imagine that dead Sinatra's voice lives on in a neighborhood drunk, then we can also imagine that the crooner sought out the voice of Frank Sinatra. Perhaps he needed Frank's voice to collect change to purchase gin. Between the living and the dead, intentions are muddled. The living and the dead and even the otherworldly are interdependent here. New agers, Buddhists, vegans, spiritualists, readers, friars, Rastafarians, wiccas, elders, and healers all make the connections. Everyone else, mindfully or not, is part of the balance, the living factor of the city's ongoing pulse.

The park stands in the center of my corner of the city, what I call Philadelphia's bazaar. More than a marketplace or a shopping street or an industrial area, the bazaar is a place of grand and tactile endeavor. It contains a web of motorheads and metalworkers and fabric wholesalers and spiritualists and disc jockeys and saints and fishmongers and tattoo artists and produce men and millers and gypsum makers and pork processors, bread bakers, nail polish suppliers, monks, food distributors, iron men, butchers, and ravioli makers. These are people on top of other people with others below them. They form layer after layer of labor, deceit, and hope.

Philadelphia's bazaar is a square formed by four connecting streets. The streets awaken each day in sequence. In the bare light, produce men come out on Ninth Street. Forklifts move stone, while loading docks fill and pickup trucks stand three deep on Washington Avenue. One by one the fabric men and women appear on Fourth Street, coffee in hand, pulling the metal grate chains and disappearing for the day into dark rooms crowded with silks and cottons, blends, gold tassels, felts, and Egyptian prints. By noon, even South Street awakens and the whole of the bazaar is engaged. Come evening, when the pink neon buzzes silently on Ninth and trash men make their way from dumpster to dumpster taking away the rot of the day, South Street blows and shakes like a mighty wind.

Here in the bazaar I learned to recognize and appreciate the city's pulse. I remember a humid day in July when the sycamore trees began their annual shedding, when the crunchy bark broke free and floated to the brick sidewalk below. Enormous crates of pale green watermelon sat in the sun. The street literally pounded with skin and breasts and sweat and incense. All around I smelled butchering, scaling, and rot. A group of black girls in tight shorts leaned over a takeout window. They must have been blasted by grease and grizzle. I saw men dragging rolls of velvet the color of morning glory. I watched their old metal scissors cut strips of gold-tinted fabric to be given as samples. I listened to the buzz of the tattoo artist, bzzzz like a loose wire, the same sound as a metal sander on a car fender. I watched a dark-skinned man hosing down a crane and pieces of bright, cut sheet metal rattling in a tray. Staring at those small pieces of metal, I imagined the hole punching on a penis, lip, tongue, or belly button. Later, as mass was starting, I sat in the back of a pink cathedral. I discovered that confession is taken downstairs near the shrine of the saint.

We who inhabit this place give ourselves to it as an offering. In life and death, we are the blood that flows through its veins. In turn, the bazaar gives us energy, basic human nourishment. We consume the smells, the closeness, and the voices. We bathe in each other's endeavor, soaking in it, absorbing it, but still we crave more.

*

One winter night, my housemate and I decided to go out for coffee. Though we are close friends, our relationship has become circumscribed by the walls of our house. Her social life goes on outside, mine mostly inside (with wife and child), and our paths tend to cross as one of us leaves the shower and the other gets in. Since our friendship started in the cafés of east Paris, it makes sense to reconnect once in a while in a café here. The trouble was choosing a place to go. We might have gone for Vietnamese coffee or Thai or Greek (some call it Turkish) or Mexican or Lebanese or French or Italian (an evening espresso while standing at the counter) or any number of homegrown soy latte houses or even Starbucks. After a few minutes, we chose a place with liberal smoking rules and couches, but that's not the point here. Nor is the point of this story to celebrate the diversity of the neighborhood, but the synthesizing power of the city. Our coffee choices represent the city's capacity to process the cultural history of the world. The essence of the bazaar is the layering of lives, the literal flattening of the world into an easily navigable grid.

Which is not to say that Philadelphia's bazaar is a sanitized representation of urban culture. Far from it. The city synthesizes culture, history, and time in the realm of a physical space. The rest is up to us. We search, navigate, align, and transform ourselves as the scene demands. The result is always something new and wonderful to observe. The tight spaces are an advantage. They force us to talk directly to each other. We sit down and speak to each other—and usually the conversation is engaging. Voices carry the place at 8:30 every morning in front of Café Cuong. Conversations go on as all day long hundreds of bicyclists and grease heads venture in and out of Via Bicycles. The Arabic-speaking men sit at the South Caffé for hours, the tables littered with espresso cups, sugars, cigarettes, sunglasses, and spoons. We talk at Orlando's before the first shift starts and standing in line at di Bruno's and in the depths of a low-topped room filled from floor to ceiling with rolls of upholstery and textiles. Our communication is face to face, in person. How else to mediate multitudes of languages and cultures? If I want something, I find it. If I want Marcia from Harry's Occult to help solve my problems, I go see her, talk to her, and explain. If I want Philadelphia Eddie to create a special tattoo, I find him in one of his studios, just as I would if I wanted the Anvil Iron Works to build a staircase, if I wanted mangos from Scott and Judy, or a wedding dress from Nobility Bridal.

I have learned to consume the bazaar as it comes to me, as signs and people and dirt spin around me. The bazaar is an anthropologist's delight, shamelessly displaying its secrets and wares. I find that it forces me to notice everything. I consume its variegated odors, symbols, and sounds. I devour the ugly, multicolored, and animated landscape, the visual contrast of a worn almost belea-guered street scene and the terror and excitement of people bat-tling for space. At the corner of Ninth and Washington, where wood baskets of large red tomatoes sit on a table way out in the street, cultures, people, and stuff mount all around. A few blocks away someone has engraved in the sidewalk cement *bizarre bazaar*. And they are right. It's nearly impossible here to interpret all the mes-sages on the street. For now, I simply report what I see and hear, what amounts to a condensed urban dream world.

Across the way from the tables of tomatoes, an ancient black man is hunched behind a plywood table cleaning lemons for dis-play and behind him hangs a 1978 Yankees jacket, Louisiana Lightening and all. Household items line the sidewalk. Aluminum roasting pans, NFL place mats, Chinese straw hats, and framed photographs of lions cover the spaces beside the buildings.

Below Broad Street, in the swell of the light and shadows, a dark black woman with fire-engine-red hair turns the corner. She wears an incandescent pink top and skirt and red four-inch heels. Her clothes cover only what might be required by law. I stop for the mo-ment to watch her. She drifts self-assuredly across Washington Avenue, ignoring the men, one after the other, who swirl around her like green flies. *What is she trying to do, man?* One asks to no one in particular while grinning like a confused possum. Another leans out his truck. *Sweetheart, I'll be on my lunch break in a few minutes. I'll be right in there. Lord have mercy.* And she disappears inside the Sav a Lot discount food store.

The noise here is deafening. Horns blast, a jackhammer strikes, a truck's transmission hits its gear. A cement mixer reverses. A truck filled with pickles, peppers, and tomatoes pulls up to the curb. At Mid-City Tires, there are black and gray cats sleeping under chairs on the sidewalk. There are cats inside the garage, under the lifts, on the tools. The smell of cat piss mingles with oil.

No one notices its vile odor, and in the depths of the garage the work of the day continues. On a bright white Coke Classic sign someone has written in vinyl letters, *Captain Jesse welcomes you to Philadelphia. Coke 20 oz. $13.99.* Jesse G. sells live crabs out of the back of an old, stationary truck on Washington Avenue. A line forms. A forklift moves cases of soda. The sidewalk in front of Captain Jesse's is inaccessible, covered by three-foot-high cardboard crates of watermelons. Wire shelves on wheels are filled with refined bleached white flour rolls and shopping carts overflow with gingersnaps, whose boxes are molded and bent by the wind and rain.

The man watching a small parking lot quietly sits in the sun. The shirt that covers his ample girth says, *Welcome in Peace.* The hand-markered sign above him reads: *if you don't pay you don't stay we call the police and tow you away.* The bazaar calls to me. It announces love and hate, failure. It is teaching me: accept everything, equally, without judgment. To the bazaar it is all the same anyway, just humanity, just chronic struggle, just short grotesque life. I notice a Vietnamese restaurant that has closed down and Phuong's tailor and fabrics. At Anastasi's, wooden crab barrels are piled six feet high. The blue crabs are alive, piled one on top of the other. They stretch and reach and snap. This is their end. They wait on the sidewalk with lobsters, stiff salty bacala and flies, whities, croakers, and blues. A block away, outside Variety Veracruzana, underneath dangling bright pink and yellow bear piñatas, a Korean man sells twenty-inch fans. Sitting in his lawn chair, he too waits.

At the Center City Pretzel Company, large, soft, doughy pretzels are 50 for $8.00, 205 for $32.80. The smell of the dough is sweet and heavy. On another building I notice a faded melba-colored zoning notice. The applicant is George D. Lapsley. The application is three years old. *The request for the selling of produce and poultry and slaughter of live poultry.* George's stand, neatly built of two-by-fours and

Astroturf, is empty. It has never been used. A Vietnamese man sits a few doors down smoking. In one hand he grips a bottle in a brown bag. He wears a green felt hat and construction boots.

Outside of Café Bah Le, Le Vo, its owner, hung a giant Eiffel Tower. Inside he makes the family's specialty, famous across the U.S. and Saigon, *banhout chalua*, pork patties. *Banhout chalua* made Le Vo rich. Each of his daughters owns a store somewhere in the U.S. This one sells ten thousand small, home-baked baguettes a weekend, and a thousand pounds of pork patties a week, each neatly wrapped in banana leaf and tied with twine. Pork is the base of their business. They make French ham and sow, snout, ears, pork trimmings, and pig liver pate, *banh bo*, pork steamed dumpling, and Vietnamese quiche with pork, noodles, and Chinese mushrooms. The quiche is glazed with egg. Harry, Le Vo's son-in-law, stacks his products up on a counter that overflows with plastic-wrapped and boxed foods. Everything is designed to be taken home, the pork chops and grilled beef over vermicelli, grilled pork and pork patties steamed with Chinese noodles, pork on a stick with shrimp and sugar steamed then fried, clear gelatin, rice, ground pork and mushrooms, sticky rice with pork patty. Harry's foods are bright green, glowing like transmission fluid, exaggerated orange, and yellow the color of aconite. They are made from coconut and monk bean, sticky rice and rice flour, tapioca and banana, sweet seaweed and lotus seeds. I take *ca phé da* to go in a Styrofoam cup and drink it with a straw.

Something like fifty thousand Vietnamese refugees have come to Philadelphia since 1975. In South Vietnam many of these refugees, including Le Vo, owned small pushcarts. They sold the southeast Asian version of the *sandwich des oeuf et fromage* that you might eat while strolling the Tuilleries. They slathered their baguettes with pate and filled them with *banhout chalua*, sow pork, and *jalepeno*, onion and cilantro. When they arrived in Philadelphia, these refugees found the hoagie, an Italian sandwich of pork and salami, proscuitto and provolone, oil and vinegar, onion and pepper, also on a long crusty roll. Now, in the cafés along Washington Avenue, we eat the Vietnamese hoagie on Italian bread from Ninth Street.

This is the scene from Washington Avenue. The city's heart beats heavy. I cannot help but sense mountainous success and abrupt failure. The bazaar gives us everything so openly and unprotected. And we in turn consume its offerings. Cash is the sole, simple currency here. There is no credit or plastic to hide behind, no corporate conglomerate. We either have it or we don't. If we aren't able to muster the cash we might never get that permit to slaughter chickens, we might not get past the unions or the Italian mafia or the Chinese. Our whole personal operation might go up in smoke or worse. If we have the cash, the bounty comes cheaply, but it comes only that way, in bulk. Strawberries are five dollars for a flat of twelve pints. Or maybe free at the end of the day. But we don't even ask for just one pint or two or eleven. The bounty is the bounty and that is that.

*

The contemporary western city—and Philadelphia is not much different in this regard than most large cities in the western hemisphere—has the power to condense people and their diverse cultures into a single space. In the bazaar, the turf belongs to no one and to everyone. At once, South Street is African, Caribbean, Israeli, punk, hip-hop, African American, and gay. It is the place for travelers, strolling families, drug addicts, college students, and old hippies. Fourth Street has twenty-odd Jewish textile houses and African American tailors. Forbidden Arts stands next to Corrupted Image Records next to Wilk's Fabric across from Armed and Dangerous. Everyone is represented—and in spades. Washington Avenue has fifteen auto repair and body shops, six tile warehouses and show-

rooms, eleven hardware stores and millers, five nail and beauty supply houses, four stone and marble cutters, five iron and metal work-
shops, and five Vietnamese supermarkets and wholesale food
distributors. And Ninth Street has fruit and produce, but also bread
and cheese and fish, beef, pork, and poultry, dry goods and dresses.
It is Italian by birthright but Vietnamese, Chinese, West African,
African American, and Mexican by inheritance. The languages spoken in the market on a Saturday morning, counted together, might
represent those of two-thirds of the world's population.

Yet the bazaar is not merely an unplanned world's fair, where
every culture has its own discreet "house" to show itself off. It's a
living, activated, potent place. Danger is a real factor of this po-
tency, of course. There is hatred in the very struggle of the bazaar. If
you win, I lose. And if you are different, it might be easier for me to
hate you. But the numbers in the bazaar don't allow this hatred to
take shape. There are too many tattoo artists for prissy neighbors to
condemn and too many forklifts for Buddhist monks to curse and
too many African American tailors and dressmakers for any racist
to deny. What is more remarkable is that the mixing of cultures,
ideas, and views is fluid and constant. Where the Italian ends and
the Vietnamese begins, or where the Cambodian begins and the
Vietnamese ends, is incomprehensible. Traditions in the bazaar are
passed down, sifted through a human colander. Ultimately they are
open to all takers, interpreters, and improvisers. The city forces us
to share space. We end up sharing time and culture. The result is a
new and ever-changing culture all our own.

*

Tens of thousands of us live in and around the bazaar. We are pri-
marily Cambodian, Laotian, Vietnamese, Irish, Italian, and African
American. We inhabit a place that is well worn, but in a constant
state of repair. We live on Washington Avenue, a broad and indus-

trial street with a distorted web of tracks converging in the center. We live a few feet from the propane dealer and upstairs from the Buddhist Temple, just outside the infusing and unsubtle odor of the New World Shopping Center's brown dumpsters. We suffer jackhammers and spilled oil, the reverse—beep beep beep—of the cement truck and the call of the banana man. *Five pounds one dollar! Buh-nanaaas! Who needs buh-nanaaas five pounds one dollar.*

We hopelessly update and alter our row houses. On every tiny street of the bazaar, on Titan and Darien and Fulton, on Ernest, Marshall, Annin, and Iseminger, charm has been redoubled and distorted. In the teens and twenties, homeowners added Mediterranean roof tiles, installed curved windows, and covered facades with fancy orange brickwork, tile, and terra-cotta details. No home was complete without a fancy iron balcony outside of the second story windows. Then the salesmen arrived, first with metal siding and fiberglass awnings, then perma-stone and vinyl doors. They covered traditional cornices in metal, obliterated bay windows with siding, and effaced brick with the morbid perma-stone. Fake gray masonry converted many a two-story row home into a castle.

But the redecorating is never enough to eviscerate the past. The fact is we live as if in a Victorian cemetery—designed for strolling and observing nature. We walk among the dead. The bazaar has always been a great, endless, row-house immigrant slum. Since the early twentieth century, Italians, Jews, African Americans and Poles have predominated. Many of their descendents remain, living in their grandparents' houses, working in their great-grandparents' stores. They reinterpret the scene of course, selling espresso instead of produce, selling imported fabric instead of making it themselves. All of us spend our lives strolling streets built by the dead, sleeping in buildings erected by the dead, continuing traditions started by the dead. Their presence humbles us, quiets our ambition but also accounts for the immediacy. When we recognize our inevitable mortality, we are free to embrace every sensual moment, to live in time. In a generation or two or three, of course, we will be the dead. Our collective unborn children will walk among our shadows.

The bazaar is volatile and exhausting. All its noises and smells and people are a distraction, a red herring of sorts that keep our hands off the true pulse of the place, the patterns of life and death. It helps to see the bazaar as a pagan deity. It is the earth and the seasons. While boundlessly sensual, it commands us to worship life and also to acknowledge mute death. When we listen and follow its teachings, our hearts open. We accept the city's immutable beat.

Once I recognized this pattern, I began to see evidence of the dead everywhere, in buildings and granite curbs, in cemeteries, memorials, and shrines. I found powerful occult formulas, saints, and blessings. I heard voices in the rain.

Standing amidst walls and sidewalks and chimneys of worn red brick with the sun glaring white, I look to the cemeteries that flank Fourth Street. The worn gravestones are covered by smooth, tall grass. Their engravings are all but indecipherable. The bones are sheltered by ash, crab apple, and gingko. The crosses here are stout and thick. The Indian chiefs were buried here: La Gesa and Apautapea and Bigigh Heautons and Barkskin and Grand Joseph and Hapeet and Tuma and Little Elk. They came to Philadelphia in 1793 on a peace mission at the call of President Washington. They came to negotiate border disputes. They died of small pox. And here they are held eternally, with colonists, slaveholders, Victorians, and warriors. At St. Peter's on the left, the remains are hidden from the street by a wavy brick wall. Inside the gate I notice a large red sign. It holds an invitation, a reminder: *These doors are open to you.*

Death is the open milky bosom of the bazaar. It flows sweet and steady. The jittery bazaar runs on in pursuit of itself, in constant reconstitution, in remembrance. The danger here is real of course.

Death is rooted in the machines, in the pollution, in the salty greasy pork, in confrontation on the street.

The dead haunt and heal the living in the bazaar. On the hottest day of the summer, I find St. Rita and her church near Broad and Washington. She is the saint of the sick and tortured. She murdered her own sons to prevent them from avenging the murder of their father. Rita prayed her way into the Augustinian convent at Cascia, Italy, took the divine wound, and died years later. For centuries, her body lay unchanged and untouched, as it was at death. Her national shrine is in the basement of this Philadelphia church. A statue of the saint displays the wound she suffered from her own crown of thorns, a bloody cut that gave a grievous odor.

In 1900, as Rita was beatified, the story goes that she sat up and opened her eyes. Construction workers and mechanics and laborers from Washington Avenue pray to her at lunch in the red, rose-covered basement shrine. They come to Rita, the father takes their confession, and they pray. The red candles that surround her statue burn for the hopeless and the sick. Upstairs, I listen as the friar with a slight accent of Boston or New York starts the mass. *Brothers and sisters we come together as a holy family.* Outside, Southwark Metal Manufacturing Company workers are on break, their giant stitching machine idle. They stare out from the cool darkness of the shop to the hot, beating midday sun. *Forgive us our sins*, implores the friar.

On South Street, in the shade of a pear tree behind the PhilaDeli, is the memorial to Cap. Fashioned from Cap's lawn chair, the memorial is an aluminum construction with plastic handles, red, white, and blue woven nylon, and patches of duct tape. *In the memory of CAP R.I.P.* appears below his picture. *Bye-bye to a special neighbor*, it says in the border of the photo. *We'll miss Cap.* Someone placed a carton of Marlboro Reds on the chair. *One for the road Cappy*, they scrawled in black marker. There are offerings of mums, freesia, carnations, and roses. And on the sidewalk in front of his chair, his friends placed a takeout cup of coffee.

We all honor the bazaar's dead. We speak to them. We cry, plead, and pray. Every week in the *South Philly Review*, we fill pages with personal notes to dead relatives and friends, remembrances, grief-knocking utterances, public moans of private hurt and pain, plain poetry.

> *It's a year now that God has taken you away from us and "our hearts" are still broken, they will be forever broken . . .*

> *Although we've said goodbye to you, we still see your face. That dimpled chin, That funny grin, Sweet memories time cannot erase for we share a love strong, we will never be apart and you will always have a special place deep within our hearts.*

The faces on these pages are often young. It is nearly impossible to look away from these family photos: a tan young man with a shit-eating grin and bright white teeth. And just below is a photo of a woman who is slightly older, but who never made it to the drinking age. She looks confident, contemptuous, difficult, and beautiful. Their deaths are special and especially moving. The bazaar accounts for its young dead. It exposes them in particular remorse, without restraint and sullen denial. The bazaar holds them out just as it draws them in, alive, to its carnival dangers and street misery. It bellows and howls for them. And each week there are more.

> *Tom, its been 18 long mos. And I just can't get what happened to you out of my head, it seems like the pain is gone for you, but it hurts so bad for me. Just knowing on this very day 8-24-2000 I should be thinking about what to do or give you for your birthday, instead all I can do is think of all the good times. God allowed us to have together,*

*and the unjustice of what happened to the murderer that the city of
Brotherly Love covered up for and why? Tom if my days are shorter it
would only be for the care I've had for you.*

These are the everyday angels that hover in the bazaar. We walk
on their streets, drink in their bars, and breathe their air. We wait to
join them. In the meantime, we rely on prophets and healers. In
trouble, we come to them. They make connections to the angels on
our behalf. They offer gifts and prayers so that we might understand the power the dead have over us.

When South Street was lined with sophisticated Jewish department stores, Harry Seligman, the pharmacist, unleashed the occult.
He found room for the spirits. He gave them a voice below. He mixed
secret formulas from ancient texts, calling on the *ifas* and the goddesses and the *yoruba* saints, the shaman. That was 1917. He aimed
to help and heal. Seligman practiced white magic only. Harry's is
the grandfather of magic on South Street. Others followed him.
Ray's Curio Shop dispenses candles for any desire or problem. A
candle burns, law stay away. To aid in winning the lottery there is
Ray's Super Seven candle, which sends prayers covering the Pick Six
and the Lotto. Bins of powders offer spiritual firmament. Rick's
Spirituals and Botanicals, specializing in African magic, is two
doors down. Rick is Ricardo Obatala, a *bobalocha*, a Santeria priest.
He possesses the powers of the *orichas*, the vital force that gives life
to all things. *Oricha* spirits possess Ricardo. They mount and ride
him, spreading their power to others. Babalocha Ricardo, whose
face is long like a Ghanaian mask, heals with the *nganga*, a sacred
pot packed with the energy of the ancestors. During the healing he
froths and writhes on the floor with basil, a sacrificial bird, and
blood. Licking the bird's neck, he slides the pigeon head around the
patient's crown. He fights enemies and bad energy. He will cleanse
your home, break curses, and restore your health and tranquility.

From his main store and warehouse on Fifth Street in the Barrio, Ricardo supplies the believer with an armory of talisman, the healing ornaments of the *yoruba* god *Osain*, a personalized *ellegua*, *oricha* rattles, tools of *olokun*, of *ochosi*, of *chango*, and any number of Haitian mojo bags for money, peace, power, or love. He offers baths, *baños sagrados y baños contra hechizo y mal de ojo*. For $99.95 there is an extralarge black cauldron and another $50 will get you sacred sticks, voodoo dolls, handcuffs, and whips.

But Harry's is the Nordstrom's of magic; its service is superior. *Our aim is to help light a torch for the good to cross swords against evil*, it says in the front window display above the oils and baths and powders that they make at the back of the store. Inside the place is unchanged since Harry's nephew Jim took over in the early fifties. *Better to light a candle then curse the darkness. Next full moon August 15 12:13 A.M.*

Marcia manages the store. She is a spiritualist, broadly trained, a believer in the abundant magic of every tradition. Having felt the presence and the voice of the Archangel Michael, she practices the magic of the angels. She performs reki and teaches meditation.

Marcia helps the sick, the *impossible*, to accept healing. Without the endorsement of the mind, and an acceptance and understanding that the problem to be healed might lie deep in the murky heath of the subconscious, the oils, baths, crystals, prayers, washes and candles, the goddesses and saints, the offerings lay fallow and crude. So her emphasis is mindful readiness, openness, and recognition. In the living ribald of the bazaar, healing by the hand of the dead is obliged and appreciated.

Inside Harry's Occult, the air conditioner cuts the swagger off the overheated street. High up on the wall is Jim Seligman's fish, the eighth largest bass ever caught in Woodmere Lake. Healing tools fill every wall. Occult oils still the world. From Harry's old formulas, Marcia and her staff produce more than two thousand oils. What the oils can do! Their labels signify the magic of the pre-postmodern world: oriental love, French love, and happy marriage. Almond oil to heal the skin and lucky root, lucky heal, and lucky black cat. Confusion, break up, hold a job, keep away trouble. *Run devil run.*

*

On any day in the bazaar, there is life and not just in the powers of the saints and healers, but in every action and in every marvelous interaction. No human form is left out; bodies crush together and voices curse, and the rats must have a field day. There is no immaculate conception here. Life on the street doesn't just happen; it chases death in an endless cycle. The living bazaar is as much a material expression of those who populate the bazaar today as twenty or fifty or one hundred years previous. And the physical place—the stores, the stalls, the trash—is a collection comprised of layer upon layer fused together so that no one is truly and discreetly identifiable. Standing on a corner, I listen, and not just to the voices, but also to the footsteps, to a rusted old metal lamp as it sways in the breeze, to the music.

At Triple A Poultry on Ninth Street in the Italian Market, the sidewalk is jammed. Across the sidewalk ears of corn are open for show. Hazy plums are two pounds for one dollar. The crowd on the sidewalk wrenches tighter. Cigarettes from all directions mask the odor. A pimply faced, red-haired teenager who is unloading boxes in the back is derided for not being quick enough to help the customers in line. He is called back and forth, sidewalk to back warehouse, and at the same time two five-year-old, blond-haired girls step through the crowd gingerly, one holding a pink handbag, the other a black one. Shoppers look forward, blind, self-protecting, together but alone amidst the human crush under the rusted and mangled awnings and the bare light of the arcade.

Just south along the wretched sidewalk, a Latino don leans against a litter-filled storefront where red snapper heads six inches long lay in a barrel. The Darigo's fish man is Asian. He's thin as a rail, with a pretty-boy mustache and a cigarette dangling off his lips. Next door I pass a weathered Italian lady selling rows of shiny wine colored cherries. From behind the east side of Ninth Street, the light smacks the hats of the vendors. The street is their warehouse. It is littered with dumpsters, rotting food, brown and curly onion rinds, an orange, a cornhusk, a blackened red pepper. Below decaying buildings, men butcher meat and children run the sidewalk. Under the awning and blue tarp, the light is distorted, like in a fish tank.

Late on this summer night when I return to the bazaar, the moon is full, the sky breathless blue to black. Canadian winds banished the wicked humidity and so the air, like the sky, sparkles. On this night, summer finally seems ready to give way to autumn. There are a few stars, enough to define the sky, a gift of the postindustrial city. Everything here seems to stand out so clearly in the bare light, the moonlight catching anything it can find. On Ninth Street, the light hits the edges of the rough steel awnings. The rest of the canopy that stretches from the buildings across the sidewalks to the street is black, solid to the night. In the mangled edges of the awning, in the rust and decay, in the patches, props, holes, and jagged cuts is the endless living brutality of the place. It is silent but for the permanent odor of raw unprocessed food, silent but for the neon signs that condemn this clear night, silent but for the dangling white bulbs that cross the street in simple careless decoration, silent but for the single bulbs that hang conscripted under the awnings themselves.

Meanwhile on South Street, it is bright as a Las Vegas day. The silence comes here much later still. For now the sidewalk is flooded. People ease in and seamlessly duck out. Up above some watch from a mindless bar called Fat Tuesdays and others drift, blindly seeking trouble, along the blackened sidewalk below. Personal identity plays fast here. It wavers in the blank shadows. Flesh is exchanged and held and handled. Earlobes have been stuffed with giant black plastic circles, casting white boys as African women on the endless golden plain. Black boys play Chinese warriors; girls dress like drag queens. A Chinese girl—peroxide hair, four-inch heels, cigarette—looks like a Shanghai prostitute and another, Korean, wears geisha makeup. We pass a white girl dressed as a Mennonite slut. The sidewalk thickens as the evening grows darker and the silver blue light intensifies. Kids from Twenty-second and Diamond say, *wassup, wassup* to everyone in their path. Inside a bookstore, a fat, shiny man wheezes like a chainsaw, holding a girlie magazine close to his puffy face. Another, a younger man in a chartreuse and black striped shirt, stares at pictures of a fifteen-year-old girl grabbing herself. Outside, I weave through slender pretty girls in purple makeup eating nachos, sipping margaritas, and smiling their corporate smiles.

Still, a group of Arabic-speaking men sits at a white plastic café table. They have multiplied and so have their cigarettes. To punctuate the maddening incongruous collection, two large black women walk past. They are dressed in full black Islamic garb. They are completely covered but for their eyes as if off the streets of Algiers. They see but never recognize the men. They are dressed for Islam, but they speak no Arabic. A block down, the night lulls and rocks, and six or seven skateboarders surround a representative of the Philadelphia Water Department. He has opened a manhole cover. They stand over him, staring, concerned, and silent. For some reason, someone believes that a baby alligator is trapped down below.

3. CALM THE POUNDING HEART

CONSIDER the death of Elijah Tucker and the birth of his grandson Paul: a single death and several months later a single birth. In the life of the family at 818 North Forty-second Street, these two events came swiftly, jointly. They produced shouting and pain and blood. Elijah fell accidentally down a flight of stairs. Paul took a first breath in a stale, antiseptic hospital room. To the rest of the family, Elijah's death and Paul's birth formed a single event. *Paul was born to bring joy to the grieving family.*

In 1971 when she delivered Paul, Sarah was fourteen years old. Sarah sensed her father Elijah in the birth room. Did he understand now why his life had ended so suddenly? She understood: if her father had lived he would have been so angry she was pregnant that he would have beaten the baby out of her. *Elijah died so that Paul might be born.*

Looking back thirty years we envision Elijah's death and Paul's birth. From the moment of his birth, Paul's own pulse became part of the city's. His slight body, his first utterance, Sarah's clear sweet milk—his nourishment. Philadelphia in 1971 was violent and ragged. Imagine the buses traversing the city then. Smell the belching brown exhaust, a diesel air infusion. Paul's neighborhood, a place called the Bottom, was lined with brown Victorian houses with wide porches and turrets on the fancy corners. Long, low cars painted olive, mustard, and gold filled the streets. And there was music, a vibe. It was the time of urban cowboys and neighborhood activism, of heroin and poetry and funk.

Some 2,700 people were born in the city that June. Others came from Kansas, Beirut, Ponce, and Shanghai, from the Punjab and

Pottstown. The city rose into the hands of each one of the new ar-
rivals in June 1971. It rose to meet Paul, just as it held on to Elijah
and all the others who came before. Thirty years after his grandfather's death and his own birth, Paul still craves the city. Yet that
same city had nearly crushed him. It had pushed him down to the
cold ground, nearly killing him. Just as he has shaken the beating
ghetto street, he has joined it. Paul's story is an intimate struggle
with the city, with the brightest forces of life and the most disturbing powers of death and hopelessness.

Paul has spent thirty years absorbing every thrust of this city's
heart, and everyday he has tried to shake free, to define his own life
and the measure of his own heart. As I find comfort in understanding the nature of the city's pulse and discover a context for my own
life in the beating street, Paul seeks boundaries. He has faced the
consequences of the terrible street. He doesn't want spiritual comfort but control. To survive, he needs to temper the city's racing
heart, the pulse that explodes inside him.

*

Sarah stayed with Paul in the hospital room up from the brown
river and the weed-knotted tracks for five days. On the sixth, the
nurses reluctantly let her leave. Paul held them rapt as any baby
might. Their hands and eyes were drawn like magnets to his walnut
skin, skin that glowed like Elijah's. It's possible that the nurses
loved and wanted to protect the bright and assertive Sarah. Sarah
fiercely protected Paul. She nursed him. She shared her bed with
him. Their bond was complete.

Paul's father was seventeen. He picked them up and brought
them to a small apartment he had rented a dozen blocks away. But
Sarah was never comfortable there. How could she have been? The relationship was hopeless, the situation impossible. A year later, when
Sarah delivered a second child, Raymond, the relationship fell apart.

Sarah left with Paul and Raymond. The cramped row house on Forty-second Street was another ten blocks north from the hospital. She carried her babies there. The house—three bedrooms, one bathroom, and a couple of couches in the front room—already held her mother and eight brothers and sisters. Now it contained Sarah and her children too. Sarah would leave Forty-second Street from time to time. Teenage love is like that. But Sarah never stayed long with Paul's father. After a while he simply disappeared.

In the 1970s Sarah often collected assistance. Still living in Elijah's house, she raised Paul, Raymond, and later Maurice and her own brothers and sisters. Not yet twenty, Sarah had eleven children to mind. Her own mother, Paul's Grandmother Carrie, was often out, gambling or playing cards in someone's smoke-filled house. Sarah held things down at the row house. Aunt Athena's husband James talked about Vietnam, about boot rot, about how the war stole all the black men. He was right. Some did return to the neighborhood, but fucked up, and the neighborhood, really the whole city, as it once was known and understood, was now deeply scarred, schizophrenic, and wild. Paul, like any child of the Bottom, absorbed all the talk and music, all the pride and anger. He internalized the triangular blocks and dead end tracks, the shuffling feet and decrepit infrastructure.

In time, Sarah had enough of her mother's house. With her three children, she searched for more space. They rented a house around the corner on Brown Street and later at Fifty-eighth and Woodbine. For a while at Fifty-third and Haverford they kept a small store. Paul's nightmares started then. In them, little repo men, sharp as needles, would sneak upstairs and then back down, hauling the furniture out the door. *Hey! Where are you going?* He would reach out to stop them only to be pricked by the needlemen. Off they would go.

Paul, Mommy, Raymond, and Maurice and now another, Matthew, laced the neighborhood. Together they were caught in a tangle of relentless poverty, dirty clothes, and no lights. Sarah worked demeaning jobs to make something, anything, possible. As they shuffled across the Bottom just trying to stay on top, the Junior Black Mafia took hold over West Philadelphia. The Bottom was becoming violent. And to the oldest of Sarah's children, it was frightening.

Paul's school, Martha Washington Elementary, was practically inside the Mill Creek project. The low rises looked like jail cells and the high rises were yellow-gray and moribund from the beginning, like something out of Communist East Germany and the relentlessly depressing Brandenburg winter. At Martha Washington the principal had come directly from the military. *Freeze!* He would shout in the hallways like that disciplinarian hero from Patterson. *Walk! Don't run!* He gave detentions freely as fights broke out in the classroom, the bathroom, and the schoolyard. Paul watched the violence gather like a dust storm across the prairie. He felt his own horizon darken.

Paul also watched men court Sarah. He learned to size them up quickly, to resist those who showed fatherly affection just to win her over. In his eyes, the men came like the seasons. They rolled in on a terrible, forceful wind of passion or gently, quietly, as companions and caretakers more than lovers. For some time, Sarah was married to a man named Malik, and then they were Muslim. Paul learned Islam, every inch of the Koran, and attended mosque and kneeled for prayers. Malik was a leader in the Islamic movement, but also a street hustler, an alcoholic. Paul remembers him as a kind drunk, but mean sober. Malik struggled for Allah, desperate to cut the drink. Malik gave Sarah stability and food on the family's table. She delivered three more babies, Rafael, Malika, and Aquila. Paul remembers feeling comfortable. Mommy was less anxious. Would Islam be the answer for the family? Would it hold the brutal street at bay?

Paul was like an open wound absorbing his Philadelphia. The street infected his blood. It polluted his air. But he always understood that the city was more than the Bottom. He sensed Sarah searching. Malik was a Band-Aid. After a while the adhesive must have worn off. One side was pulled away from the skin and the wound was exposed again. Paul was bewildered the day they left, not by the act of leaving, but by its severity and Mommy's silence. There they stood, six children, three bags, and the number ten trolley. At the Greyhound bus station downtown, Sarah waved a wad of cash in front of the ticket window. *How far will this get us?* Sarah didn't speak to Paul or the other children on the bus. When they arrived in Richmond, she had no money left. They slept at the Y.M.C.A. Sarah was twenty-four and Paul was ten.

The Greyhound bus was freedom from the crushing streets of the Bottom. It was freedom from the pulse of drug dealers, the Koran, the projects, stories of Vietnam, men on the corners, well-intentioned school principals, and the winter wind that beat stark trees against her bedroom window.

Eventually families took them in. Paul thinks it was some kind of charity. They stayed on a ranch and then with a Jewish couple named David and Sara. The couple bought the children new clothes for school and toys. Mommy kept all six in line and well behaved. Their host Sara told Paul how much she loved him, how she loved them all. One day she proposed to adopt all six. Mommy would be the family's maid. Sarah ignored the proposal but the childless woman insisted and meanwhile spoiled them more. When Sara's determination became unnerving, at Mommy's will they were out on the street again.

With Sarah's new boyfriend, Steven, they were eight as they finally headed north. Sarah had tried, but she could not shake free from Philadelphia. Their hungry city took them back, a reclamation, no explanations. Sarah searched for stability for her family, but now the streets of the Bottom bounded with aggression and no matter what your game—for good or bad—it seemed as if anyone might snap at anytime. Drug dealers owned the corners and the alleys. Drunk men, filthy but wise, stumbled in the darkness and spoke clearly perhaps only to warn, *Don't go there.* Between the pushers and swill bellies there was mutual distrust but also understanding. To each the other fit the scene like a creek to a forest: not interdependent but part of the same basic lexicon. On certain blocks, ugly girls led men into rotting houses and took them on braised red shag rugs. They burned fires inside and poked veins. Some never left these houses with wide gabled porches—porches covered with char and heaps of wet clothes and pink plastic headless dolls.

Mommy returned to this scene with six children and Steven, who had never lived in the big city. They took a row house on St. Bernard, under the El tracks, the asphalt below glassy black as if it were permanently icy. It was cold in the house. The first winter, the pipes froze and burst; the electricity was turned off. They boiled water to take baths. Mommy took welfare and Paul began to notice.

At Martha Washington, Paul fought to keep away trouble and to protect Raymond who was right behind him. He turned in straight As and earned acceptance to Masterman Junior High, a city magnet school, the best in the entire state. Here was another opportunity to escape the suffocating, swelling ghetto street. It would be three-quarters of an hour to get there each day, but he would leave behind the dreadful, binding neighborhood and the menacing fear. Maybe the rage that was budding inside him would wilt and die. Each morning Mommy would send him out across the city to be with other children from other neighborhoods and he would share their vast experience. At the end of the day, the El would leave him at Fifty-second Street in winter's darkness amidst dim storefront windows. He would return to her. She would see him change, and he would watch her.

But he didn't attend the magnet school. Paul didn't take the El every morning and then the trolley to the number seventeen bus to Spring Garden Street. The city didn't yet give bus and subway tokens to students. Mommy had six children to feed. No room for luxury, no smart kids' school. She enrolled Paul at Sulzberger Junior High School, two blocks from the projects and Martha Washington.

She enrolled him there, but he couldn't get in. He couldn't skate past the gangs who demanded payment. They blocked every path. To get to school in seventh grade Paul Tucker was forced to evade the Hoop Street Gang and the Market Street Muggers and the kids from the project. With Raymond still at Martha Washington, he was alone. At Fairmount and Forty-eighth he was forced to pay or be beaten or turn around and go home. But that was not an option.

Even as a boy, Paul was an observer. He watched everyone, Mommy especially. He internalized her weariness and also remarkable energy. Then, when he left her for the day, and as soon as the gangs came at him, he watched them. He recognized their solitude and sadness. But still he took a beating. He gave away his change and he went in. Day after day this same ritual was repeated. Once he understood aggression, he fought back. He turned so completely that he frightened even the older boys in the gangs. Possibly he had observed too much. The miserable punching, scraping, kicking, and biting came straight from the heart. At twelve, Paul was in danger. To everyone around him, he was the danger.

They placed Paul in shop and in other basic classes. The books were dirty and old, the teachers uncaring. His clothes were *bummy*. He was skinny. Everyone teased Paul Tucker, the girls especially, and he wished they were boys so he could beat them and make them go away. That was his solution—beat them and they will go away. When a gang *bumrushed* him in the hallway, he would bite the leader or pop him with his elbow. He figured that if the leader was hurt and incapacitated the others would back off. Paul would be left alone on the hallway floor, in the school they called the Jailhouse on the Hill, in the neighborhood they called the Bottom.

When he scored ninety-nines on the assessment tests, he saw white people inside the school for the first time. He remembers them looking over him like a science experiment, the black genius. *Why is he here?* he heard them ask. *He's violent,* they answered, not hearing the question, so the white people left as suddenly as they came. They left the skinny boy in the infernal schoolhouse but moved him to the eighth grade and the smart classes. The nerds flocked around him seeking protection, but mostly he remained alone, and prone.

Meanwhile, Sarah watched Steven being pulled to the neighborhood's play. He too, the sweet older man from the South, was becoming violent. He began to beat her. She tossed him out. But the house was a mess even without the violence. The electricity was cut off as much as it was on. Paul feared Mommy too might fall into the neighborhood's swill and terror. Paul watched his mother react to each day, to scarcity and pressure and disaster so constant it was routine. At night in the dark house, she lit candles and in the candlelight she read aloud to the six children. The flickering light and Mommy's voice and the stories calmed him. Sarah harbored her first son in her confidence and steady love, and to him she alone was home. She was his neighborhood, his house, his street corner, and stoop. She was his goddess.

Steven had been banished from the house, but there he was in the house one day. He and Mommy were fighting. Paul and Raymond could hear the shouting, and when he hit her they jumped. When he was there earlier in the day the police had been called. They left, though, without stopping the aggression. This was a domestic situation after all. But Steven came back. When the boys heard the sound of flesh striking flesh, in that instant they went after him. Paul and Raymond chased Steven, but he escaped. The brothers returned home and with their mother jumped into an uncle's Aries K car. When he finally saw Steven, all Paul felt was terror and fire. The neighborhood supplied the brothers their weaponry. They picked up bricks and pipe, a cane. Their brutality didn't last long, but they were thorough. Their anger overwhelmed the man. Paul and Raymond fractured his skull, busted his legs, and broke his ribs. They crushed him, this boyfriend gone bad. Deep in a trance, the barely pubescent boys pounded the man.

They pounded this city that pulsed inside them. Paul after all was bound to this city, bound by birth and circumstances, bound by his eyes and nose and ears. He had absorbed so much that the weight of it all nearly crushed him. The beating released the weight. With each punch he was lighter, freer.

The lightness evaporated in the moment. *Freeze don't move.* Fear built in the police car. It poured through the vinyl seats and back and forth from Paul to Raymond, older brother to younger. Trapped behind the Plexiglas, they were shackled and pale and weightless. At the Youth Detention Center, Raymond braved a question. *How long will we be here?*

Forever, motherfucker. You nearly beat that man to death. Raymond lunged toward the officer and from then on the boys were separated. Mommy too was thrown in jail. They became known as the violent brothers, bad seed. They were the only inmates whose arms were tied. Days disappeared as they awaited a hearing in front of the judge. But when the hearing came, Steven didn't show. The charges should have been dropped, but the judge showed no leniency. He called a second hearing. Steven never came. Eventually, after a month bound and ostracized, Raymond and Paul were released. Back on St. Bernard, back in the Jailhouse on the Hill, Paul could not suppress his rage. The other students feared him. Now *he* was the needleman of their nightmares. Say the wrong thing or look the wrong way or play a joke that's not so funny and you would pay. Prick! And watch the blood.

*

Paul was in a box. Enraged, he punched the air. He kicked. He squirmed and flailed his arms, but he couldn't get out. From inside the box he would never have the capacity to mute the pulsing ghetto. He would never learn that the city also gives life, that it might charge him with righteous energy as much as it now deadened his spirit. Yet somehow Paul saw an opening. He credits his mother with the ability to show him the light—despite the pervasive shadows. Sarah never stopped reading to the children by candlelight. Paul knew instinctively to listen, to watch her as she read. Paul saw beauty, courage, and love. The darker it became in the box, the more she helped him see. They stayed up late together and talked. She taught him all that she knew. Sarah was not yet thirty but to Paul she was old and wise, the wisest. Sitting with her he recognized something beyond the box, something lush and uncertain. He did not know what it was or where it lay. But he could recognize its thundering cry. It beckoned him from the ghetto.

In a forceful, blowing rain, he and Raymond walked out of St. Bernard and under the tracks. Yellow lamps glowed like floating globes. The water from the rain greased the gray granite curb. It flowed east to the river and the university and the center of the city. Under the dripping El and the clank of the subway cars, Paul imagined a forest and a cold stream glazing bitten rocks. He imagined what he had never actually seen, which only made the vision that much clearer.

Now the boys jumped the turnstiles. Up on the platform the gray enveloped them. The city below was hidden by the mist clinging to the red brick and trees and domes and steeples. But he knew it was there and for the first time, Paul realized that all of it could be his. Paul came to understand something about the pulse of the city that only Chinese medical practitioners know about the human pulse: it is not one rhythm but many. He knew at that moment—thanks to years of his mother's determined teaching—to seek out life and beauty, the sustaining thump-thump-thump of city life.

When high school came, Paul Tucker left the Bottom. He chose to attend a school in North Philadelphia. Dobbins Tech was not a bad school, or perhaps it was merely not ferociously cruel like Sulzberger. The books were old at Dobbins, pathetically out of date, but the teachers were committed, at least to trying. The thugs there didn't know him. At first, he felt a certain safety in being unknown. Then he realized he would have to craft everyone else's expectations of him; there would be no time to waver and let it slide.

Each day he left St. Bernard Street on the El. It took him from Fifty-second Street. On cold vinyl seats, he traveled in and out of a brown tunnel and was deposited on streets he did not know. Carrying his scars with him across the city, he took this new route to escape not as some sacrosanct act of purification, but as a mapless hiker takes a fork in the trail: he closed his eyes for a moment and heeded some faint urge. But Paul sought not mysterious, wild beauty. He just wanted a slight incline where, at the top, the view might be less obstructed. He came to high school this way—not prone but sagacious, almost strategically, searching for an opening in the mist.

As much as Paul sought freedom, he could not escape the violence. On the gym floor, when he felt slighted or provoked his instincts took over. He scratched a boy who then shoved him hard from behind. *Oh, you want to fight?* A signal went off inside him and he wound up and uncorked a right, right to the boy's mouth. The boy screamed, *My mouth, my tooth.*

Up in North Philadelphia, fighting was commonplace, especially between Dobbins and its rival Simon Gratz. Gratz students were outlaws terrorizing the Broad Street Subway. At Lehigh station, they robbed Dobbins kids' sneakers, coats, and earrings. The boys from Dobbins banded together to stop the pilfering and in the center of Broad Street, fifty boys were at war.

He spent late nights with Mommy on St. Bernard and asked questions and listened. She explained the female body to him, and sexuality. It was not until then that Paul noticed girls, and even then, in a poor high school, he had to look a little harder. Beauty was not always so obvious. He was turned on, anyway, by odd looks, girls in glasses. And together, Paul and Mommy explored religion. They searched for a comprehensible god.

As high school played along, Paul learned to suppress the particular rage of the Bottom, or at least he tried. Paul placed it somewhere outside of his thin, wiry being. He placed the rage in poetry, in rap—and left it to his dreams. As he slept, inside his head Paul was being chased. He ran, not wanting to deal with the pain, hoping to escape the cruelty and aggression. But it always ended the same way. Paul turned on his own dream. He turned on what was hopeful and pulled the gun himself. He ended the chase.

But rap was his hope. It was evidence of his experience, of the street and the beauty that seeped through the mist. Paul bled indignation into his songs, and then he hid it in something pretty, in popular rhymes, in girls and cars and freedom. In flaunting. But no matter what he said, his voice was clear and it claimed for him space in the city, the space of his own creation. By the time Paul performed at the Dobbins' showcase, a few of his friends had begun to call him Royal P. Graduating Dobbins, Royal P had a record contract in hand.

*

At times, Paul found himself back in the Bottom, in a place he detested, where he felt mostly shame and depression. Corners were filled with stacked tires and white-and-almond-colored appliances.

Cloudy lightless taverns served their invisible patrons. Former Episcopal, now Pentecostal, churches were flushed with worshipers on Sundays. A basketball rim hung bent and sagging from a telephone pole in front of no one's lot of brown grass. A sign read, *no dumping*. In the front window of a small row house, hung a shrine to African Americans with a giant picture of the martyr, Malcolm X.

One of Paul's first girlfriends lived on Girard Avenue, around the corner from his grandmother's house on Forty-second Street. Paul was there among the graceful houses, the bay windows painted brown, red, green, mustard yellow. It was a chilly day in November. The sycamore trees were white against the gray street, their long branches reaching out over the trolley wires and the tracks below. After some time inside his girlfriend's house, he left. She followed him as far as the wide nineteenth-century porch. He went out on the avenue.

Then a man on the street spoke to him, saying something Paul couldn't understand. He was accusing Paul, or so he thought. *What?* Paul asked. His girlfriend was still there on the porch.

Don't run, I got a gun.

What's the problem? Paul threw the elbow punch, sharp to the chin and the gun went down. They scrambled. He remembers his girlfriend watching, frozen. She did nothing. Another man and a woman, a girl really, tall and thin, approached them on the sidewalk. Paul shouted out to his girlfriend on the porch. *Do something. Go get your brother.* Still, she was frozen, or, he thought, unwilling.

Now they numbered three on Paul as they dragged him a few houses up and onto a porch. The thin girl pulled another gun. The girlfriend's brother arrived, as if by chance. *Let him go. He's my boy.*

Step back. I'll blow your head off. It was the thin girl. And to Paul, *I'll blow your dick off.* They pushed Paul inside and he tried to convince them that he was not who they were looking for. But the tall girl re-entered the apartment this time carrying a shotgun. Her nostrils were wide and eyes empty. She came toward him. Paul fought for his life. He kicked and bit and grabbed her. He hit her. He saw clearly her washed-out eyes and he knew that she would fire the gun.

She did.

As she shot, he pushed the gun to the side. She ran off, and he saw black. When he came to, one of the men was patching the wound in Paul's side, where the bullet still was lodged. He stopped the bleeding no sooner than the cops exploded through the door.

Paul fell in his own neighborhood on a street he never thought much about. A block away is the Cathedral Cemetery. But for the quickness of his hand, he might have ended there.

Now, sitting at home recovering from the gunshot, with pellets still deep inside his flesh, he wanted desperately to burn the whole place down. It was a familiar vision. He had seen it in his nightmares. For months he rarely went out, afraid more of his own reaction, his own reflexes, than of anyone else on the street. He sat and he dreamed of revenge, of murder, and destruction. He felt his body fill with terror, fear of himself, of his own ideas, of wickedness and sadness. For someone who had narrowly survived a random shooting, Paul felt no relief. Instead he was numb.

He and Mommy talked about spiritual strength. She coaxed him out of a fatalistic blur, away from the suicidal street. She forced him to keep the rage at bay; she forced him to talk, to release. The more he talked, the more he loved her, his saint, his Sarah. Craving vengeance eventually wore thin. So they wondered again if there might exist an appropriate god, a god of ghetto rage, of street play and innocence. Who could be their god?

Paul found an answer, the best answer at least to casual bleeding on the floor of an apartment in West Philadelphia during the reign of the Junior Black Mafia and crack cocaine. He found the only answer to a place that so severely pulsed with death and insensate ritual, with numbness, blindness, exhaustion, and setups and tricks. He wanted, at nineteen, to have a child and Stephanie, his girlfriend, agreed. When Sarah came, little Sarah, his twisted mind unfurled. She was beautiful. Paul saved his life by having a child, a girl he called Sarah, like his mother. To have Sarah was to say, despite everything, I can give and I can love. To himself he gave a daughter, named for the only person in the world he truly loved. To this daughter, he gave the city. Paul was shot and Sarah was born and the city felt a tremor, a shock of life.

For both Sarahs, for his saint of a mother and angel of a child, Paul always returns to this city. When Sarah was born he was out on tour for the first time, in New York performing for teenagers. As soon as he heard about his baby girl, Paul grabbed the next train from Penn Station, he tore away from his newfound world and the attention and the rush, and he went to the hospital to hold his baby girl.

Paul brought Sarah into the world only knowing that he and Stephanie would do their best to protect her and to keep her from the shattering terror of the street. Paul's deal with Diamond Records put him out on tour again and out in the developing culture of rap. Money was fast; egos raged all around him. He was gone half the year becoming the rapper Royal P, and money became his shield of protection. They lived comfortably and without fear.

Somebody moving
My car system
I like 'em loud
My car system
Rocket proud
Girls come around because they can't resist 'em
That is the sound of my car system

He cut videos and maxi-singles, and through his voice he shared pure indignation with his followers. Royal P was not rapping about his car radio but his humanity. When he said, *my car system*, he really said, *my heart*. *I exist, a young black man* and no one can deny it. *My heart beats*. Deal with it. *Forever mine*, the girls in the background sang.

> *I don't drive a Benz*
> *I'd rather take a Lincoln*
> *When a cop stops me I know what he's thinkin'*

Out on the road, on a twenty-city tour, the buzz made Paul hyper. The crowds scared him, all those hands reaching out, touching, grabbing, tearing at him. They caressed his hair, tore his jacket, all these girls. At once he was overcome by adoration, stardom, and fear. He had never before been farther than Richmond and this time he was not just a boy from the Bottom, but a man from the 'hood.

He played Compton and found the heart of the matter. Rap was there and for a moment so was Royal P, a skinny boy from Philadelphia. He had never been so excited or afraid. He wanted to resist the gangsta life, wanted to reject the guns and drugs and women. He came home then bewildered by the scene, trying to stay clean. He came back to Philadelphia and Sarah, whose feet he always smelled first thing, a father's joke. He and Stephanie decided to have a second child and this one would be a boy, he knew right away, a father's ancient claim.

They were a family of four and Paul was just then old enough to legally drink. He had confronted the monster of his time, the unnerving pain of the performer, of the boy out in someone else's 'hood. He left clean. No one pushed him too hard; he never snapped. In the city, he stayed off the street, avoided unfavorable situations. He raised his children. Around this time he saw a cousin who had nearly been mugged on Fifty-second Street. He owed his escape to Paul, or rather to the legend of Royal P. *P is my cousin, you know Royal P.*

Hey, no disrespect, and the booster returned the watch, the cash, and the cousin's jacket. *You tell Royal P no disrespect.*

Some months later Paul left again to go on tour and it was the same drill, only worse: bodyguards and easy egos, hands scratching. The scene was overbearing. He performed with Snoop Doggy Dog, showed up in Compton in a limo. He performed behind a locked gate. He saw violence and drugs; he saw the money handlers and little room for creative expression. To Paul, it felt like Fifty-second Street, crude and muted and dangerous. He had to get out.

He had spent four years as a rap star, and back in Philly he still had a little cash. Paul was alive. He had his own children. Paul had lifted the immeasurable distorted burden of the ghetto. He was free from the daily pounding of the street. Again, he came to a crossroads. After quitting rap and still feeling a creative pull, a calling once buried and now unearthed and fed, he attended art school and learned graphic design. Meanwhile, he and Stephanie grew apart. He could have left then and started over. He could have taken a new name. He considered living in Miami, Atlanta, or California, putting Philly away and keeping it there, buried. This time, he would choose his path, with a map to guide him, the map of his own experiences and of his own confidence. Never again would Paul feel the rage, the viciousness, or the pain.

Mommy had an idea, a vision. She wanted Paul to see to it, to publish a fashion magazine, by and for and about the women of the city. She wanted them, after all the time and struggle, to have something of their own, about their city, about reality. *There can be beauty in reality, right?* And Paul wanted his family to see that beauty, without having to look as hard as he did. Sending money from a far-off city was one thing, but if he stayed in his city he could show them the beauty himself. He wanted to face the whole campaign of his life and stare down the evil. Look long enough and everything softens, becomes a blur. From the blur he decided to form a life of his own creation, in and about and for *his* city. It was the only way. So once again, he returned to the ghetto to start a magazine, at a center that would help him do it. The city, *his city*, needed him, needed his determination, his voice, it demanded all that he had absorbed. He went back under the El tracks where he had first surveyed the kingdom. Standing outside, he stared across the tracks. The hard steel that was composed against the grace of the wide, grainy sky vanished in the stare. It was all inside him now.

Mommy had taught him to stand up and let no one block his way. He knocked the gang leaders down and made it to school, and he cleared a path for all his brothers and sisters. He stood up hard and accounted for himself and gave himself a girl named Sarah and a reason to live. He stood up and turned around and walked away when the rap scene deteriorated and aggression stomped all creation.

Mommy offered to put up the cash for the first issue of the magazine with her savings from a successful house cleaning service. She opened the door and Paul became an entrepreneur. He threw himself and his life and everything he remembered into it. Paul Tucker became the magazine. It was his reality, ghetto included.

The first time the magazine came off the press, he held a party and fashion show in a museum by the river. The huge room was filled. Photographers surrounded the runway. He said then, *I am a magazine publisher*. A woman in chartreuse graced the cover. The first issue was thin, but it was his bold statement. He *was* a magazine publisher. He held the party at the edge of the subway line, fifty blocks from the house on St. Bernard. Royal P was a publisher, the only black, former rap star, publisher of a fashion magazine in the country. The magazine held his promise. *I am You*, it said on the cover, you whose breasts are not large enough for *Cosmo*, whose skin is too dark for *Harper's*, whose belly is too large for *Vogue*. I am you, he said again that night in the large glittery room above the sailors' museum. Mommy was there behind him, and she must have drifted way up to rafters, her dress inflated with pride. The night was endless, nearly perfect. Even the second rate models burned the cameras that draped the runway.

And he thought then it would catch on, this magazine that prophesized the beauty of every woman, of the street, of the city itself. He filled the pages with the city, with the whole of the rusted, muted place, with its pain. In a fashion magazine! On page thirteen of the first issue was the magazine's simple cry and credo. Beneath a photograph of a contemplative, powerful woman out in the light-braised night, it said in orange letters: *every woman*. He pushed this concept hard, pushed the looks and the lighting, pushed it out onto the street and into factories and cafés and bars, in courtyards, and in empty lofts. He covered a woman's naked body with thick black latex and placed bracelets and a watch on her wrist. In the photographs she held out her arm as if to dare the boosters that might swarm around her, as if to demand the thorny passion of the street itself. The women on these pages were never easy, fragile, or simple, but always strong, commanding the air and the sidewalk and the worn wooden floor. They were never perfect and sometimes brutal and sometimes blurred.

The buzz held through the preliminary work on the next issue. But the project faltered. Mommy financed the first issue with her savings, but the cash did not last through the party. The second issue didn't make it past the printer's door. It was a long year with a gray, warm winter, and Paul had only an orange prototype of issue number two and out of date looks to sell on the street.

All along potential backers and advertisers said to him you are publishing a black fashion magazine. They never asked, is this a black magazine or even is this a fashion magazine? They believed they saw the ghetto itself before them in the lanky rapper whose front teeth are spread, whose left eye wanders slightly, whose chin is covered from time to time in dangling fuzz. They saw the ghetto in the young man in the suit, and they took his magazine from him and handed it back; they saw the ghetto but not the city. They saw a young man off the street with his black magazine, grainy lunging photographs, and city moods. They said, for a black magazine, this is groundbreaking. They saw the young man, an old rapper called Royal P but not Paul Tucker, who said, I am a magazine publisher. At once they tried again to put him in a box, an ugly, blackened ghetto box. But in the ghetto, you find a way out of the box or you are dead.

They asked again, why not just print a black magazine? You know you can't compete with *Elle* or *Vogue*. They asked again, why don't you take the magazine back to the neighborhood, put it back into the brown printer's box, keep it there in the darkness beneath the El. Theirs was the old fear rising, the fear that once grew thick in the Spanish oaks, the fear that held in the humid air and inside the white-washed antebellum mansions. Theirs was the fear of black Adam and bone-pure Eve, the fear of the field-strengthened slave and long glances, the fear that charged pathetic hatred and left men by the hundreds hanging for show from rough, bent limbs. The publisher dared to show white women and Asian and Latino and black together or apart. Here was the beauty of Paul's city, the whole city, from his perspective. No, he explained, *my ghetto is not enough for me anymore*. The city that now pulsed inside Paul was vast. Its old walls were coming down.

*

In three years the magazine has not generated much revenue. To put out each issue after the first is for Paul a blood sacrifice. He styles the shoots, works late into the night designing the layout. He has no capital. He is faced with roadblocks and other people's fears. He is challenged and denied, kept outside the mainstream, kept out. He is politely hated. He feels hatred like most people feel the coming snow on a day when the sky is dense, almost yellow. At times Paul feels the rage return in one demonic instant. He watches it build. He holds it and warns and warns again and then he explodes. *Hold it, you don't know me. Don't let my suit and tie and little shoes fool you. I want you to know, I am telling you with respect I am going to rip your fucking head off and piss down your fucking throat.* But Paul knows that as he pushes his magazine forward, pushes his world and the collected experience of his life out onto paper for others to read, he will have to control the anger inside.

Sitting in a tight gray carrel, Paul is remembering. He looks trapped. He keeps the rage at bay. He leans back in the chair and then forward, for a moment he's hidden by the partitions. His smooth, puffy hands are wrapped around his head. The phone sits unused. The walls around him are painted in bright colors. Out in front of him sits a list, but not his list. This is what his business advisors would like him to do: not publish a magazine, but instead make a living designing logos or brochures. He doesn't listen. He can't waste any more time. He has no money and no financial backer and he owes. There have been lawyers and ideas that have come and gone. He printed three more issues in three years. He made plans that were never executed. There have been fights and threats and compromises. He juggles, and his vision has sharpened in the turmoil. But Paul is grounded by a lack of resources. He has a new issue set up a floor below on the bright screen. But will it ever see paper, the newsstand, the reader? He knows that to pull it off he will have to extend himself beyond the limits of his own force and vision. He is left to wonder if that will ever be enough. For months, Paul bounces in this limbo, completing the magazine's layout, selling ads, raising money, though never quite enough. He is a single person in the city, but leave or stay, rap or publish, what he does matters. He is a part of the place. And like the story of the city itself, his outcome is unknown.

TWO: BODY

4. THE BUTCHER SHOP

IMAGINE an immigrant's butcher shop: white tile, a tin ceiling, and thin red blood. The butcher bought the building just a few years after he arrived in the city. He proudly wrote his name in tile on the doorstep. *Tenaglia.* He raised a family in the apartment upstairs. After fifty years in business, the old butcher has decided to close his shop. His grandson has no interest in wearing a bloody apron all his life. On a Saturday morning a slight breeze catches the yellow leaves on the tree facing the butcher shop. One by one, they drift to the sidewalk. They become tangled in the windshield wipers of a blue Ford. They pile in a gentle circle under the tree. The butcher, wearing a white T-shirt over his round belly and a wool cap on his head, stands behind his counter. The store is empty but for tools and cases. A radio is set to an A.M. station. The voice of the newscaster is hollow and tinny. On a thick piece of white paper, the kind that he had, until the week before, used to wrap chops and filets, he writes in black marker: *Store for Rent. Ring doorbell at left.* He tapes the paper to the window.

Months pass before anyone inquires. In the spring a young woman asks to see the store. She bakes fancy wedding cakes in a place a few blocks away, and as her business is growing, she wants more space to meet with clients. She loves the tin and the tile floor and the white cases. He rents the store to her for three hundred dollars a month. He sells the stainless meat hooks to a guy who will sell them to an antique store. They will hold heavy wool coats, soft merino scarves, and yellow rain jackets next to the door of someone's capacious postindustrial loft.

The baker does well in the old butcher shop. She hires an assistant and she places ads in thick sweet-smelling bridal magazines.

She paints the store creamy yellow and the door pink. Neighbors stop in for scones and coffee. They bring the newspaper and in spare moments, she sits down to chat. The air around the old butcher shop has become dense and sweet.

The baker is popular. In order to keep pace with demand, she realizes that she needs two more ovens and several more hands. In just three years, she has outgrown the butcher shop. The baker moves one block away. Now in his eighties and his wife in a nursing home, the butcher asks a realtor to sell the building. He will move in with his son. The new owners turn the butcher's house into two smaller flats and the butcher shop/bakery into a studio apartment.

A middle-aged man with no family and a love of early Kansas City blues moves in. He tends geraniums below the old storefront window, now cleverly closed up by glass bricks. The pale north-facing light can enter the apartment, but on the sidewalk, we can't see in. The man lives there for ten years, bringing in the geraniums at night and back out in the day. The red blooms warm the steely January street. He dies of cancer in his eleventh year in the apartment, from too many Camels perhaps. He dies playing Ma Rainey. Later in the year, the landlord finds a new tenant, a tall thin woman with the same pack of Camels, jet-black hair, and a solid silver ring poking through her navel. She notices the antique terra cotta pots below the window, the thick Japanese branches of the plants. She thinks, well maybe I can sustain them. Lacking experience in looking after anything green, she waters them too much. The pungent spicy leaves turn yellow. Worried they are drying out, she waters them some more, and they die. Weeds grow rapidly in their place. In winter the weeds turn brown and wet. Plastic bags and q-tips, a grease-black sponge and a water-soaked tissue gather among the dead weeds.

The old butcher shop is one building in a city that contains a million. This one-time house to an immigrant butcher has three stories and is made of brick. It boasts bay windows, tin ornamentation on the cornice, and wood floors. A building just like this one stands in every neighborhood across the city. It is like a tiny freckle on an immense body. Placed together with all the buildings around it, and the streets and parks and monuments, it is the physical proof of our existence. As human beings have arms and legs and torsos, necks and heads, cities have buildings and avenues and waterfronts and neighborhoods. The body of the city is made of these inanimate things but we inscribe them with personal meanings. We inscribe our name on a doorstep; we paint a door pink. We inhabit the city's body.

We become intertwined with our cityscape. Day after day we animate its streets. We alter it so that it represents our tastes and values. It becomes our personal idea of a city. Immigrants paint murals to represent their homeland. They plant traditional gardens on abandoned dirt. They open cafés like those they remember in Abidjan or Lushenjë or Nice. Neighborhood activists boot drug dealers from a park. They grow trees there instead. Artists colonize an old market street. They build studios and gardens, a world of their own creation.

But no one in the city is God. Not even Robert Moses, at the height of his powers in New York, wiped the slate clean. The Babylonians could not erase Jerusalem. When the Jews returned to the razed city, they held the destroyed temple, palace, and neighborhoods as sanctified space. They incorporated the area as a monument, connected to their new city. The immigrants, activists, and artists that we imagine to have colonized streets and abandoned lots and parks did not inhabit empty earth, but the body of a city long modified by generations before them. Some might consider the abandoned dirt where immigrants created a traditional garden to be the unformed body of the city. But it is not. It is the product of the evolving ideas that determine, at least for a while, the city's fate. As a vacant lot, it is a representation of someone's values, an idea of the city—as a wasteland—at a certain moment in time.

Our immigrants and activists and artists place their own values on the space around them, on top of or next to others already living there and those long since gone. The immigrants paint a mural on the wall of a corner building much like the butcher's. The building was built eighty years before the mural was painted. The mural painters do not erase the builder's intentions. They are simply adapting them. As they do so, the city's body evolves. It changes form, texture, shape, and complexion.

Standing under the tree across the street from the butcher shop, we watch the building change. We note the smallest traces. We identify smells and colors, flowers, trash, building materials, and signs. At one moment the brick is painted red; at the next, the red has been washed away. We watch the building carefully as the days and months tick by. We watch it like a long still shot in an art-house film. We watch people settle in the building, claim it, and commit their lives to it. The building represents them on the street. It contains their passion and endeavor. We can imagine the scene as it was in 1927: a man in beige work pants is bent over the doorstep installing one-inch hexagon tiles white but for the name: *Tenaglia*. The tile man is like the tattoo artist writing a lover's name on a biceps. We are watching an act of love and ownership.

As time passes, someone covers the tile; even later, perhaps someone else will demolish the butcher's building. But his life remains, for now trapped in the walls of the building. We look carefully there. We find his wife's dining room wallpaper, a paint color he chose for their bedroom. Inside the storefront, now the studio apartment, we find the tin walls and ceiling that contained every atom of energy of this man's working life. It contained his knife skills and his joy and the lessons he taught the neighborhood boys who spent afternoons working for him. And after a demolition crew knocks the building down, and the brick and plaster, wood, marble and tin pour into the basement below, the butcher's life will be contained in the dirt, in the very foundation of the city's body.

We place extraordinary meaning in the body of the city. The ancient Jews called their city a princess. They extolled her beauty and perfection. She embodied the purity of their law. When they were exiled they held on to her image. Though crushed and mangled, they wanted her back. Their belief in God was not enough to sustain their religion. To survive, it needed a sanctified place, a body. We talk a great deal about placelessness in the United States, about the lack of a meaningful landscape. But the body of the city, to paraphrase Walt Whitman, contains our multitudes. It contains and reflects our individual desires. The butcher spent the better part of his life in the three-story building with tin ornamentation and bay windows. He worked there day after day, slept, caressed his wife, and held his children and grandchildren in his broad arms. As he grew older, the building and the block, even the street trees must have crushed him with familiarity, with commonplace beauty. He must have heard voices, seen ghosts on the street corner, imagined conversations.

The city's body inspires us. Buildings catch the setting sun; they glow in the moonlight. Sounds of children bounce off sidewalks, alleys bring us shadows. The air is saturated with concentrated human energy. Every inch of the streetscape provides clues about someone's life. We notice posters glued to a wall, now partially covered by other fliers. One advertises a sidewalk sale. We can read the words *moving, children's clothes,* and *bedroom furniture.* Another poster is mostly covered—all but the perfect part in the hair of a candidate for mayor. The details of our lives overwhelm us, we see them cast in stucco, granite, and brick.

Of course each of our relationships with the body of the city is distinct, a function of who and where we are. I find that certain places engender certain types of relationships. Some places harbor us. Others seduce or repel us, or even make us feel ambivalent. As much as we like to control our environment, the place itself can dictate. In a sense, the result—the tangible, physical city in any given moment—is a collision between ourselves and the physical stuff—houses, streets, and trees—that we find there.

On Baltimore Avenue near Forty-fifth Street is a two-story building split vertically into two sections. On one side lives a family from the Côte d'Ivoire. They run a restaurant on the ground floor. On the other side, a Sudanese businessman and activist has opened an insurance agency. One is West African, the other East African. About 2,500 miles apart, their countries both span the tenth parallel. Here in Philadelphia, they live on either side of an old wall. The wall separates them; they establish their own communities. The wall joins them too; they share space, confront the street together. The avenue harbors them and thousands of others from Africa, Asia, and Europe. It harbors so many different people that none try to own it. They simply come for freedom and protection, perhaps to establish their culture in America and then, as has been the pattern, to incorporate it and move on. Once they do, the avenue accepts and protects those who follow.

As much as the avenue or street or neighborhood in the city can serve a constant function, it also changes. Some of us wish to seize a spot and make it our own. Middle-class African Americans set out in the fifties and sixties to possess a neighborhood called Germantown. They wanted their own Gold Coast. To a degree, they have been successful. It is now a comfortable, even thriving place. Yet sections resonate ghetto more than gentility, because none of us are powerful enough to completely possess the city. None of us can erase the history of the street. Nor can we still the city's constant motion. Yet we grab on. We place ourselves in its hold. We bind ourselves to the immense figure. We burrow our heads in its chest, run our fingers through its hair. Each of us shares the pleasure and disgust, each of us like a tattoo artist, inscribes our name in flesh.

5. THE AVENUE

I **COME** like an immigrant on a hot summer day to the avenue. I am searching, but not for peace or bread on the table. On a summer afternoon, I wish simply to observe the sweep of time. I hope to capture a single moment, a clear picture of people in a place.

To get there, I take the Baltimore Avenue trolley, the number thirty-four. It skates gingerly through the subway tunnel. It shrieks a piercing whine as it turns, edging slowly south, underground. At a red light, the conductor waits for the car ahead to move along. She brings the trolley up to the stop, and it heaves back and forth like the exaggerated top hat of the circus clown who rides the unicycle. A few passengers step down and disappear into the station. Several people, dark figures really, sit waiting for the trolley. None board this one, though, and it shoves off, lights blinking, ahead.

The trolley car is all but empty. An exacting light appears as it emerges from the tunnel. The sun is high and strong. Inside the car it is cool, the air bland and stale, faintly unpleasant, like a doctor's office or a library. Eerie, oddly ominous sounds echo in the car: each time the motor pulls and creaks, each time the door opens and closes, each time a passenger requests a stop, each time change is placed in the fare box.

I arrive on the avenue, just past the statue of Charles Dickens. The warm air outside the trolley is enveloping in this leafy, streetcar suburb. Unlike the bazaar, this is a forgiving place: roomy, broad, and planned. This is the chest of the city, a haven and shelter. Up above, all around are signs of the Victorian well-to-do: white stone turrets and painted shingles, wide porches, Stockholminspired roof designs, columns made of brick, little love seats built into the woodwork of the porch.

Despite the calm luxury, there is a torrent of people. They come to the avenue from Africa, from Asia, and from the Caribbean. They come all at once, nestling, planting, and transplanting cultures. Immigrant life is a long, infinite moment. The avenue's refugees are struggling to join a certain America, or not. Some are able to cast aside old ways. Others simply clasp tighter to their own traditions, waiting to return home. Either way, they are compromising eternally with themselves and each other. The majority of immigrant life is hidden from the street. They have created small, parochial worlds, interior, insulating barriers. The barriers warm and guard and ease the uncertain transitions. Baltimore Avenue indulges them. It accepts them willingly. It carries their smells, displays their colors, and like a good parent favors no group above the rest.

The refugees share, in the words of Sudanese insurance agent Siddiq Hadi, a readily apparent respect for each other. Each person on the avenue knows why the other is there. The specific reason, whether political, economic, or religious, doesn't matter. Just outside Siddiq's office, Sudanese men, women, and children and families from Nigeria, Liberia, and the Ivory Coast, those who came to Philadelphia from Ethiopia and neighboring Eritrea, from Jamaica and Korea, and even Bulgaria, mediate and share a single space in a single point in time. Many own businesses and houses along the avenue. Although they don't own the avenue. The neighborhoods around Baltimore Avenue are solid, traditional African American territory. In the center sits the great and influential Hickman Temple where Reverend Patterson, who wears the ring of an eagle on his hand, presides. It is also a neighborhood of progressive scholars and activists associated with the surrounding colleges and universities.

Here I am too, just off the trolley, wondering if the avenue will indulge my notebook. Unsteady at first and untrained, I wander up and down. Without listening closely, I struggle to digest the scene. Starting where Forty-fifth Street intersects Baltimore Avenue, I catch glimpses. A Laotian family serves dinner in their corner garden under a blue tarp roof that covers their heads. The family's chickens, whose red headdresses glow in the gold light like the coals of a fire, waddle down to the street oblivious to their urban plight. Careless, they step in dirt and oily grime. The family's voices grow louder. A girl wearing her Catholic school uniform comes out from inside the makeshift fence. With clunky black heels she attempts to guide the chickens inside, but they ignore her and she gives up, faintly.

Across the street in a barely lit social club next to the *halal* market, Southeast Asian women play cards in the front window. A set of Big Wheels sits in the open doorway. A thick heavy odor of starch—the smell of cooking rice—blankets the street. Music comes from both sides of Forty-fifth. With the door open, rap bumps out of a small row house while on the west side it is Gospel, large and full and furious. Jeeeesus! Down one block, a deeply beautiful, chocolate-colored woman in a red *chador* walks past the white and green mosque where Sudanese and Lebanese men are talking in Arabic, and where the girls wear blue skirts and keep their heads covered. A long-featured Ethiopian man sits on a blue and white nylon lawn chair outside a restaurant called Abyssinia. On the chair next to him, open and folded down to keep the page, is a paperback copy of *The Grapes of Wrath*. Opposite, two awkward boys learn karate inside the International Shotokan Karate Association, their parents talking, not really watching, under fluorescent lights. Outside the Second Mile Center, a thrift store, stationary bikes, a high chair dating back to 1966, and dingy old furniture line the sidewalk. Inside the window I find a plastic place mat that explains the weather. *Cold air from the poles sinks and flows down toward the equator.*

Past sunflowers and red firecracker plants, a house painted blue
and yellow, sit hippies and activists and travelers drinking coffee
and reading old papers outside Sam's market. For hours they sit and
read and talk around makeshift tables, a scene of dogs and dreadlocks. At Sam's it is impossible to tell the customers from the staff.

Baltimore Avenue sparkles this Tuesday late afternoon, with the
sun high above the immigrant collective. All around are deeply ex-
pressive buildings, but the sidewalk is empty and silent. And Mr.
Hair, whose red and stainless barber chairs can recount the history
of black America, is closed for the day. The New Third World
Lounge, where the roof leaks like a colander, is still and shuttered
until night. I notice a vacant lot, a perfectly manicured garden,
birdbaths white and gaudy as swans, multicolored chrysanthe-
mums a month premature, and God's Rescue Mission. *All are welcome!* Above, posted on an outdated billboard: *Ghostface Killah—
Supreme XX in stores Feb. 8th.*

Return the land to those who use it! I read the leaflets that cover
an abandoned building. *Die nazi punk. The party's just begun.
Twenty-eight thousand Abandoned Houses (according to the Department of Licenses and Inspections); seventy thousand (according to
housing activists). There are over twenty thousand homeless in Philadelphia. If every homeless person in Philadelphia were given an entire
building for themselves, there would still be thousands of abandoned
buildings left over. Rent goes up when those in control of shelter create
an artificial scarcity of houses. The less there is of it the more valuable
it becomes.*

The street poetry continues on the avenue in the infinite
American delirium, everybody and everything, all at once. Mes-
terem Ethiopian food, Mariposa Food Coop, Leroy's Showcase
Lounge, and Dahlak, for the islands in the Red Sea. Fu Wah Grocery,
Queen of Sheeba, Amigo African Market, Joe's Choice Meats,
Tony's Barber Shop, Baltimore African Market. Ox tail, goat meat,

stockfish, and hard chicken. Dried fish heads, farine de banane, Ovaltine, and Klim, the brand of dried milk.

This is Baltimore Avenue on a Tuesday in August at the beginning of the twenty-first century. It holds its refugees suspended somewhere between birth and death. It holds me, searching, waiting for others, for more human lives, more stories. The avenue waits, placidly, open and available. I oblige, now understanding. I will listen to the others around me. To do so I must caress the city's body and insert myself in its folds.

Inside Abby's Desert Lounge near Forty-eighth Street, Cynthia the bartender wears a low cut Lycra shirt, white striped sweatpants, and bleached gold hair. She is trying to tune out her best customers, three old timers: Bill, James, and Gary. It is Bill's birthday. Sitting in the cold dark bar he has just finished two tall glasses of whiskey. Cynthia is trying to watch *Divorce Court*, but Gary is turning down the sound of the television. Bill puts Coltrane on the jukebox. Everyone in the bar but Cynthia would rather listen to "A Love Supreme" than the idiot on the screen who claims that his wife had lied to him about her age. Seems she was older than he was led to believe.

Bill has the kindest, strongest face a man could have, and in a straw cowboy hat and tight white T-shirt he appears like a seventy-five-year-old god. He wants to make a point about marriage and divorce. He claims never to have been married. But if ever he did find the right woman, he would be true. He stands, arm bent, then points to the bar, *I would be true to her for the rest of my life. Uh-huh*, says Cynthia, ignoring him. A sign on the wall announces, *the Party's Here*, and Gary, who is thin like a gangly teenager, slips in a joke. *One hundred years ago what did they call a bunch of white guys chasing a black guy? KKK. Today they call it the PGA.* Meanwhile, Bill, the resident Descartes, could not be stopped. *Thousands of books could be filled with everything I don't know*, he says staring toward the bar. *The older I get the dumber I get.* The paneling is dark, the ceiling covered in tile. He looks around at his friends. *I'm more proud of these guys than Tiger Woods.* He toasts them, holding up his glass. Bill runs the bar, vodka and gin, whatever. We soak up the cheap liquor and darkness in this bar owned by a man who came from Ethiopia. All of us inside are sheltered from the sun. Will the paneled walls remember this moment when we have forgotten it?

We all oblige the avenue with our laughter, with sweet saxophone, with our legs dangling below the lacquered bar. The men who inhabit Abby's during the day own the place. They decide the music and handle the remote. They open the door for newcomers. But there are no gatekeepers on Baltimore Avenue. It stands ready for all of us, one after the other, or all at once.

*

Moussa Doumbia sits on a sun-drenched lawn chair outside his restaurant, which he named for his daughter Fatima. He wears a yellow and blue checked shirt. Benkady Fatima is in the two-story building that also houses Siddiq Hadi's insurance agency. The two are next-door neighbors. They share a brick and plaster wall built nearly a century ago, when European powers ruled much of Africa and the Middle East. Moussa lives above the restaurant with his wife Koro, his daughter Fatima, and his one-year-old son. His eldest daughter lives with her grandparents in the Côte d'Ivoire.

The other dark men who stand talking outside the restaurant are well dressed. Their phrases spill out languidly. Certain words are drawn out. *D'accord* is said, not in the dispassionate Parisian way, but like it means something. West Africans add extra syllables to their adopted tongue. *Ou est elle? Elle dors.* Koro is sleeping upstairs. The Mandingo men stand outside to the left of the door, toward Siddiq 's office. And Moussa looks ill. His eyes are red-yellow and his skin is rough and puffy. He is sick, hepatitis or something worse, and everyday, I am told, he is becoming weaker. Moussa is a pillar in the West African community. Among the Mandingoes, the kind and warm Moussa is an immigrant hero, self-taught and self-made. His restaurant is the center of West African social life in Philadelphia. During the day at least, it is given over to men. They sit, very often alone facing the kitchen, eating oxtail stew and rice. On Saturday nights hands and arms reach across tables, touching. The country blue room fills with laughter, with fried fish and plantains, sweet and thick.

Later in the week I search again for Moussa. A man leads me up the brown weathered staircase at the front of the restaurant. Koro and Fatima, who is nine years old, are watching Spanish television, a variety show called *Cristina*. Abdul, thirteen months and huge, a giant train wreck of a fella, screams for his mother's attention. But she is intent on the show, sipping a mixture of *sirop de menthe* and milk. Her nails match this concoction, a pale washed green like the walls of a formal living room. Moussa, I learn, has left, gone back to Côte d'Ivoire to be treated for his illness. Koro speaks quietly. Fatima translates. On his first day there, Moussa was so weak that someone had to carry him to the bathroom.

Moussa had sent for Koro once he established the restaurant. Now, after two years in Philadelphia, Koro speaks little English. She relies on French and Mandingo, on her own people for support and friendship. She spends most of her time caring for Abdul or helping out downstairs in the restaurant. She struggles to find day care for Abdul, even a few hours so that she can go to school and learn English. So she leans on her daughter. Fatima learned English in less than a year. Now, she speaks three languages. But at her school, where students come from thirty-two different countries, where they speak sixteen languages, they call her a dirty African. So she plays in the park down the street with the two Korean girls next door, whose parents own Joe's Meat Market.

A half hour later, a friend of Moussa's, a man, enters the apartment, just to check in. Spanish news reports a police beating in North Philadelphia, a huge local case a la Rodney King. In French, the man and Koro discuss the case and the *droites de l'homme, la constitution americaine*. They agree that the victim, though arrested on countless charges of assault and robbery, would receive a settlement. Fatima sits bored, restless, on the couch. In the tiny room, time disappears in the rhythm of the television, in the panning camera, shouting neighbors, yellow police tape, and in the mug shot of the beating victim. To Koro, Abidjan, *une grande ville*, so busy and crowded, seems dreamy and far away. But jobs are scarce there, so Koro and Fatima sit on this couch on a street draped with others, different, but just like them, hesitantly waiting and watching television.

As much as Koro, Fatima, and Abdul fill the small dark apartment above their restaurant, Siddiq's outer office is empty, cold, and sterile. This is a dehumanizing place in limbo. I wait as dusk forms at the tops of the street trees. Music plays above, smooth jazz or something worse. I listen to every lyric, so ridiculous and sappy, so patronizing and clear. *I don't want to live without you*, groans the third-rate talent. I am supposed to believe him!

Perhaps the atmosphere is an accident of Plexiglas and white paint or perhaps Siddiq wants his back office to seem, in comparison, like a library's lounge, so comfortable and inviting. There, among the red leather chairs, bookshelves, and his brother-in-law's paintings he holds meetings and discussions on international political strategies. As an activist in exile, Siddiq organizes against the fundamentalist regime now in power in the Sudan. He also works to get medical aid to his country's suffering children. In the hollow of his office, in his house or elsewhere, he holds the meetings of the Sudanese National Rally or the Baltimore Avenue Business Association or the Sudanese Business Association. He plans a new Sunday school for the children to learn Arabic and Nubian, Islam, and Sudanese history. He teaches at the school, which is just across the street from his office. All the while, Siddiq envisions a new ethnic group in America, the Sudanese Americans, every ounce a part of the American experience, bringing with them new tolerance and openness to their adopted country.

When Siddiq arrived in West Philadelphia there were just thirty Sudanese and most of them were affiliated with the university. His brother-in-law was studying fine art here, painting large red canvases and building macabre sculptures. In seven years since coming to Baltimore Avenue, Siddiq has watched and willed his community to grow. Now there are something like four or five hundred Sudanese and most are right around him at Forty-fifth Street and Baltimore Avenue.

Siddiq's skin is the deepest purple, black, and brown, and his eyes appear like moons, wide and open to the world. In the Sudan, Siddiq witnessed beatings and torture, "emergency" trials. In jail as a dissident, he watched military officers axe the hands and feet off of other inmates. He was detained two years during the old military regime, his eyes taking all of it in, unafraid.

If his eyes had no choice but to accept the death and hatred all around him, his heart did not. In Sudan, Siddiq was a trade unionist and a human rights activist. If he had returned to the Sudan after his year working near the palace in the Sultanate of Oman, the Islamic government would have arrested him. He would still be in jail today. While he lived in Oman, the National Islamic Front—with all the oil money in the world—executed a successful coup. Activists and intellectuals left while they could. From Oman, Siddiq traveled to Florida and eventually to Philadelphia, where sycamore trees tower over houses like skyscrapers in the desert.

Soon after, Siddiq opened his office in an old stop-and-go market, once the bane of the neighborhood for its malt liquor and its wino clientele. He named his office for the Nile, and from the start his neighbors were open and accepting. He found peace, but also an unstoppable fury, an impenetrable need to cast his people into the mold of the American republic. In his darkly lit back office—walls consumed by certificates and soccer team pictures—this large framed man never stops planning and organizing. He is kept with the endless task of creating a new society for a people long chased around.

Well into the night, as Siddiq Hadi plays the music of Muhammed Wardi, Benkady Fatima fills with a French-Mandingo-Creole blur. Siddiq talks relentlessly about the history of political torture in Sudan, about a new people, the Sudanese Americans, and this, their avenue. On the other side of the wall, inside the restaurant, a lawyer discusses the legal issues regarding immigration and naturalization. The lawyer has brought American women, women looking for African husbands. That makes his job much easier.

Outside, behind Siddiq's office, rain pelts the fire escape. Brown, leathery leaves gather in the gutter. The insurance man's daughter and wife are at home, but he wants only to talk, to tell me about the Sudanese of Baltimore Avenue, about the prodigious harmony among all of the avenue's refugees. To him, each immigrant group here is like a tribe in the heterogeneous pre-Islamic Sudan. Siddiq believes that we derive value from our collective differences. Diversity and respect are common themes on the avenue. For this insistent man, no issue is more important.

By now, the lights have been turned off in the front office of the insurance agency and the phone has stopped ringing. Siddiq looks down occasionally as his mind flips from medical aid for children to the rebellion by women in the community who are demanding that the men teach Sunday school. Siddiq regularly holds intellectual salons with other exiled Sudanese. Outside of the salons, the largest debate of the year is part of the Sudan Day celebration, held upstairs at the Second Mile Center.

Sudan Day is a serious event for Siddiq and the other organizers. It is an important day filled with the furious act of defining a new culture in Philadelphia, while reaching back across continents and time to the Nile, the Red Sea, the Nubian Desert, and the plains of the as-Sudd. For many of them who attended the celebration, the Sudan is a diverse country of ancient cultures, Islam a new and overbearing bully. They wrestle with their nation's fate in a neighborhood once built for a bursting city's new merchant class. The debate was the marvel of Sudan Day. Solely men participate in the debate on the question of "Sudan as a multiethnic society." The result of the debate would be reflected in the flag printed on the Sudan Day T-shirt. Depending on the outcome, the shirt would either display the current flag of the Islamic government—red, green, and black, or the prerevolutionary flag—yellow, blue, and green. The debaters argued whether the current regime was, as Siddiq believed, much worse and more brutal than even the military dictatorship that had preceded it and whether the nation had ever truly been accepting of its multiethnicity. Not every Sudanese person in Philadelphia is a political refugee, or an activist or an intellectual. Many still support the current state and they wished their flag to dress the shirts. On that spring day in Philadelphia, at least, they didn't win the debate. These Sudanese chose a history of tolerance, of heterogeneity. They designed the shirt with four hands together in a circle and the words of the nation's greatest singer, Muhammed Wardi. *You have never been degraded in our eyes.*

Later in the night, films on the condition of women and girls in Sudan were shown on a small television. Women with bright colored clothes and traditional facial scars sat together and talked while the men crowded in groups. Before the night was over, a storyteller, Tamadour Sheikheldin, the number two actress in all Sudan, enacted a two-person play. She played both parts, condensing the entire play into a few minutes. To Siddiq 's delight,

Tamadour shouted and raced about the room, on top of the crowd and in it, one character and then the other, her voice echoing out to the street and into the spring darkness below. The storyteller's voice enraptured the room, took hold of the celebration. The genius of this performance was Tamadour playing both the widow and the spinster. In a split second she was one and then the other and perhaps the point of all of it was that they were one, neighbors dependent on one another, their fates intertwined.

What else but the theme of neighborly love and understanding might matter to a man who is helping to establish a new culture on Baltimore Avenue? As I sit with Siddiq in the depths of his office and Fatima sleeps upstairs on the other side of the party wall, lilting French bursts in waves amidst the smoke in the restaurant below. The trolley rattles past Benkady Fatima as Moussa grows weaker on the west coast of Africa. In the shelter of this colonial highway, what else might matter?

6. THE GOLD COAST

I THINK it could be argued that we all come to the city like the refugees who inhabit Baltimore Avenue. We seek shelter, community, employment, and entertainment. Fifteen years ago, I came to the city to go to college. It's a familiar story here: suburban boy moves to city, finds a true home amidst the ever-changing urban landscape. Since the day I arrived, the streetscape has levied an emotive, disturbing power, a force strong enough to enrapture me. I've spent hours walking dark alleys on wet cobblestones, drawn by the shadows cast by fire escapes. I'm perennially seduced by architecture, by the whole of the physical city. I am hooked. I want to possess it, so I buy an old house, rip it apart, make it my own. Then I look outside: my neighbors are all doing the same thing. I realize that each of us is attempting to own the city. But the city can't be possessed by any one of us. Its brilliance is a factor not of narrow interests but of its openness. Still, many of us try to take some control. We engage in turf battles, and ultimately we gain, what? The outcome is never quite what we had planned.

*

It's no more than three blocks to the center of Germantown from Tulpehocken Station. It is at its center where the place unfolds. The neighborhood reveals its layers beneath twisted wisteria and towering Tulip trees, behind stone walls, and in the mud-addled medieval street plan.

The Germans came from Krefeld, a village twelve miles from the Dutch border, in 1688. Quakers and Mennonites mostly, they arrived on a ship called the *Concord*. By standing and occupation

83

they were hermits and revivalists, weavers and tanners. Their names were thick as winter ale: Op den Greff, Arets, Seimens, Strypers, Lensen, Kunders, Tyson, Luckens, Bleiker, Keurlis, and Turner. The families strung Germanopolis along an old native path, neglecting to create a town square. Instead the unpaved trail became an open pass through, a trade route, a place of itinerants and colonists, fighters and bumpkins, Germans, Dutch, French Huguenots, English, Swiss, and Swedes. That Philadelphia was but two hours away on foot was the new colony's chief selling point.

Germantown extends northwest from central Philadelphia. It begins the chain of settlements along the east side of the Wissahickon Gorge, where a German family settled in caves and later built the first paper mill in America. David Rittenhouse, the family's prodigal son, was born in a wood cabin near the mill alongside nineteen family members. He became America's greatest astronomer.

Germantown remained the center of the German community in the New World, but only until the British asserted their influence on America. By then Pastorius and Hendericks had abandoned German and Dutch for English, and British summer cottages stood over half-timber German roadside houses. Later, the Revolutionary War over, Germantown harbored escapees from a Yellow Fever epidemic in Philadelphia, including President George Washington. Benjamin Rush, the city's leading physician, advocated purging and bleeding to stop the fever. Mosquitoes, refugees from Santo Domingo, and rotting coffee were blamed for the hazy vomiting plague.

The streetcar and railroad changed Germantown. Perfectly American vernacular Gothics and Victorian gingerbread houses were built alongside cracked yellow stucco colonials from the centuries before. Germantown was sucked into the expanding mass of Philadelphia, annexed with Spring Garden and the Northern Liberties, Southwark and Moyamensing, Kensington and West Phila-

delphia. And then as part of the great Philadelphia industrial machine, Germantown carved a particular role for itself: it became a
middle-class enclave, with tweed-coat prep schools and a progressive point of view. Germantown always had an affinity to Princeton
Waspishness and straight-shooting social correctness no doubt due
to its Quaker roots. A tolerant and modern community, it was
among the first places that blacks came to freely. It was a place to
show off and settle in comfort.

Germantown crept north in the 1920s. A new district called
Mount Airy was built alongside the gorge all the way to Republican
Chestnut Hill. The new area was filled with neo-Tudor, neocolo-
nial, and Spanish colonial houses. Collegiate gothic apartment
buildings were clustered around train stations. Like the heart of old
Germantown, Mount Airy straddled Germantown Avenue, the
trolley route from downtown and the commercial center of Philadelphia's northwest.

African Americans began settling in Germantown in large numbers in the fifties. Up from North Philadelphia they came looking
for middle-class status among the stone houses and old elm trees,
proof and prophecy that they too could share in the dream. The
idea was to escape a tiny row-house life, to create something gen-
uinely African American and rich. They were large families of
preachers and professionals, engineers and grocers. They came on a
mission. Along the way, they became attached to Germantown, to
Mount Airy, and to Lincoln Drive, their own Gold Coast.

By many, it is considered un-American to not want to escape,
advance from poverty and the old neighborhood, to get out.
Constant craving for more has defined the nation's psyche. It defines the growth of cities, as original Victorian streetcar suburbs became dense working-class districts and new railroad suburbs were
built to replace them. As those 1920s neighborhoods aged, the
process redoubled as mountains of cars spilled off the factory line.

In the story of American city-building, any place is a stepping-stone to the next. Real estate values hold sway in the family algebra.

But a significant majority of city dwellers have always been poor, held in place by high rents elsewhere or racism, poor education, immobility, and insufficient access to capital or jobs. Particularly for African Americans, attachment to certain neighborhoods has not been a choice at all but the status required by insurance companies and banks, real estate agents, zoning boards, and every fulcrum structure of American hatred writ into law and practice. When North Philadelphia blacks *chose* Germantown and particularly sections of Mount Airy, they were purposely countering these expectations. No place in Philadelphia could have been more beautiful. The Wissahickon Gorge slices a forest-in-the-city. The hilly mill town landscape of white working-class Manayunk and Roxborough sit to the west, and Germantown, Mount Airy, and Chestnut Hill to the east. The landscape is old and charming, the trees tower, and enormous rocks and caves punctuate the hillside. The forest itself is filled with stories. Wagon passages are revealed in rock scars. We know of the taverns that once lined the creek and the textile mills that were perched way up on the ridge.

Germantown Avenue lifted whole extended families in postwar ambition and dropped them on plush ivy carpets. Far from magic, the operation demanded careful attention and vigilance. These merchants and professionals were dedicated to the enterprise of black legitimacy and desired integration. Germantown would be their seat at the table. Starkly different from building a new, entirely black suburb like Forest Park north of Cincinnati, moving into Germantown meant becoming part of a place that was already well established. Could the black Gold Coast stand on such hallowed ground?

Unlike the immigrants that arrive each day on Baltimore Avenue, the African American families that first colonized Germantown wanted more. They wanted real estate. They wanted to possess the graceful body of the city, to adopt its charms, its towering branches, its creeks and springs, its gentility. They wanted to shop in the old-line department stores at Germantown and Chelten, walk in the shadow of George Washington, cruise the curving drive named for Abraham Lincoln.

If we imagine Philadelphia in the 1950s, we find a place on the cusp—it is at once willing to embrace the racial revolution and stubbornly entrenched in old ways. The city's fathers at the time were patrician progressives who sought a measure of social justice for blacks. The Quaker tradition too buoyed hopes of equality and peace. But neighborhoods were (and by and large still are) squarely segregated by race. Borders were defended with fists and knives. The black families that migrated to Germantown leapt into the tug between justice and hatred. They met slamming doors and for-sale signs just as they were offered hands to shake.

We can watch the scene through the eyes of a child. Cynthia Bayete was five when her extended family moved en masse to Germantown. She heard plans for the future. *English townhouses. Country garden. Driveway. Best behavior.* Cynthia sensed that the fervor for land was a giant step for her family. The land grab made them feel like they must prove their worthiness.

Meehan Avenue was quiet. The fine English-style stone townhouses boasted generous front gardens. Even the back alley was landscaped and welcoming. Dogwoods and cherry trees and red maples greeted the street. Cynthia's grandparents, the Reverend Daniel and Essie Barnes, bought number 252 in 1952: exhibit A in the great leap from North Philly. After they moved in, they watched the for-sale signs sprout like daisies. But not every white family left. Those who stayed saw that Reverend Barnes, a Church of God preacher who was sent out across the city to spread the word of the Bible, was determined to prove that African Americans could make a neighborhood better. He built a deck over the driveway in the back of the house. Essie planted a garden in the front. Mostly the Barnes and the other new black families were proving to themselves that once the door was open, they could keep it that way. They would not let it slam hard on their behinds. The vigilance was exhausting. The self-criticism was absurd. As a child Cynthia was told to always be polite, always upright. No transgressions were allowed. *Property values must not fall.*

Cynthia watched her grandmother Essie dig a hole for the arborvitae and carefully groom the other shrubs. She watched an elderly woman cultivate a garden, a social revolution committed in soil. As a child Cynthia knew the significance of the move to Germantown. She loved the Meehan Avenue house, her family's center, and the days spent with her aunts and grandmother and her mother. Later she realized that number 252 represented a hard-won acceptance. Almost fifty years later, Cynthia sits in a car across from 252 Meehan Avenue. She sees herself as a little girl watching her grandmother. Essie places the root ball into the hole. Cynthia understands now: the roots are her own. Fifty years later the arborvitae is gone but she is still here. Cynthia now lives in her fifth house in the neighborhood. She is bound to Germantown by memories, by cultural history, by physical beauty. Germantown is the lush body of her city. Though Daniel and Essie and thousands of other African Americans came here to make Germantown their Gold Coast, Cynthia's attachment is different. Germantown possesses her.

When Cynthia received a journalism fellowship from Berkeley, she felt no hesitation in leaving Germantown. Like many young people, Cynthia wanted to leave the nest. And more than that ordinary desire, she had started to doubt the moralistic approach of her grandparents. The fellowship was to be her first real newspaper job. Good-bye Glen Echo Road. No more family buzzing around, questioning, *What, you're leaving? Why?* Nearly twenty-seven years after her grandparents landed on Meehan Avenue, Cynthia took off to Rochester, Illinois, to work for the *Register-Star*. She never intended to look back.

That May she received a phone call. Her mother was unexpectedly and terminally sick. Without question or thought, Cynthia packed her bags. Her editor said, *What, you're leaving? Why?* In days, she found herself back on Glen Echo Road, where she had vowed never to live again. By August her mother was gone, but Cynthia stayed. Several of her aunts owned houses on the streets around Glen Echo. A couple of others still lived on Meehan Avenue. Possessed by the place, acting on instinct alone, Cynthia bought a house of her own right in between them. Hers was a white stucco twin on Lincoln Drive.

*

Cynthia calls Lincoln Drive the spinal cord of Philadelphia's northwest, the vital matter that connects the community. She sees the black experience in the roadway's twists and turns. It's an apt metaphor. A half a century later, the black Gold Coast may look the way Daniel and Essie intended. Parts of the neighborhood are famously integrated; parts are rich. Property values are rising. A fourth generation of middle-class African Americans is settling there, and like Cynthia, many are attached to the place, in love with old woods, shady gardens, and stone houses. What of the twists and turns? The pioneering African American settlers of the fifties sought real estate. They wished to own a genteel part of the city. They struggled mightily to build their dream. They wished to possess the place, to remake it in their image. But even today, their greatest possession is their *idea* of the perfect city. African Americans own little of the shopping district at Germantown and Chelten. The finest shops are gone anyway. What's left is an active and entertaining hodgepodge, at times more like North Philadelphia than wealthy Chestnut Hill.

If there is any snobbery left to the shopping district at Germantown and Chelten, it exists on Maplewood Mall. The small stores on the pedestrian walkway are exclusive. They are filled with men and women from the Gold Coast. Diane and Tom's Cafe and Linda's Cafe and Boutique have outdoor tables. Flowers grow in half barrels in front of every store. We find custom upholstery, health food, silk flowers, a music studio, and the offices of Parents United for Better Schools. We find the artifacts of Daniel and Essie's journey, but circumscribed to this small block.

As comfortable as Germantown and Mount Airy became for Philadelphia's black middle-class, as much as the tall oaks protected them and the ivy cushioned their feet, resentment, hatred, and denial have always loomed. Cynthia's youngest daughter Kamilah once returned home from a birthday party next door to their house on Lincoln Drive, having been told she could not participate in a children's game because she was black. All the other children were white. This was 1984.

Germantown is rich with early American history, remnants of it anyway. The colonial quarters of the earliest Philadelphians were here. The characters were Quakers, many of them rich merchants. Their old family houses are strung along Germantown Avenue. The houses still stand in places where Germantown Avenue has otherwise faded away, where poverty and abandonment have distorted the rest of the streetscape. They stand there protected by white suburban ladies. The furnishings are important. The china and rose gardens are meaningful, as are stories of the revolution and early American prophets. But black life, really the slave experience, has been ignored in the interpretation of these monuments. Black people have been largely kept outside the walls. A significant part of their own Gold Coast is to them a vast hole.

If Lincoln Drive is the spinal cord of the northwest, Germantown Avenue is its central artery, its jugular vein. Slash the vein and blood pours out. Examine the blood and find millions of cells: some red, some white. Put the microscope to Germantown Avenue and we find the stories of millions of people: some black, some white, some rich, some poor. Each one tries to define the place—as Gold Coast, as ghetto, as sanctified historical site. Each is trying to possess this corner of the city and none can, not completely. The city, like a lover, can possess us, as Germantown does Cynthia Bayete, and we become attached. We can grab land, but the city will always break free from our grasp and seek another lover. At best, we can learn to share the city's pleasures. At worst the polygamy repels us and sends us away.

*

I stand in front of a perfectly proportioned old stone house and my head swirls among oak, sycamore, and tulip trees. In this urban oasis, I lose all sense of direction. Germantown Avenue disappears. It's raining and the grounds envelop me in a lush late summer womb. The ancient, twenty-four pane, double-hung windows of Cliveden, the house built by the chief justice of Pennsylvania, reflect the humid forest. Statuary is moss bathed and bright. Leaves rustle above. Several wild turkeys roam in this six-acre forest. Caretakers grow giant sunflowers, nicotiana, and chiles.

For years growing up, Barbara Cooper would pass the stone wall surrounding Cliveden. She might gaze inside to look at the trees, but she never gave the place much thought; she knew she was not welcome there. Cliveden did not exist for her or most of the African Americans living in the handsome nineteenth-century neighborhood around it. Even after the National Trust took control of the property from the Chews, a bizarre self-absorbed family, in 1972, the grounds remained out of their reach.

The Chew family tree, which dates to John born in Chewton, Somersetshire early in the seventeenth century, is a flowchart of Benjamins and Samuels, Anna Sophias, Marias, Sarahs, Margarets and Henriettas, the names repeated eight generations to the grave. The Benjamin that built Cliveden in 1763 was council to the Penn family, a royal appointee to the courts, loyal to the crown but protected in house arrest during the war. His descendents kept the house as a living family shrine to their own bloated sense of importance in the history of the nation. The Chews were proud and elite. They were dreamers, protectors, Disney-like imagineers, as out of step with the neighborhood as the grounds of their family home were unknowable by the neighbors.

Their pride rested on the events of one day when Cliveden's name was called and thick October blood was shed. On the day of the Battle of Germantown, the two-and-half-foot-thick walls of Cliveden held safe the soldiers loyal to the king. George Washington's troops marched down Germantown Avenue in a campaign to retake Philadelphia from the British. They stormed Cliveden. Washington's rebels were massacred, but proved enough mettle to entice the French to join the war. As a result of the battle, the revolution was given new life—or so the story goes.

Much to the chagrin of the neighbors, the day is relived and reenacted annually. At the entrance to the Battle of Germantown a volunteer sits at a folding table. *The Americans don't win today, sorry*, she mutters. People in felt fill the grounds. I notice a boy in Christmas green and red, a camp ground of muskets, ye olde socks, orange plastic crates, fiddlers, and the piercing whirl of bagpipes. Some of the soldiers appear mangled already. At first soldiers outnumber spectators. There's a Scottish regiment with brown coats and the blue coats of Yankee Doodle Dandy. An ambulance provided by the Keystone Quality Transport Company sits and waits.

Tourists in college T-shirts and hats are the first to march down Germantown Avenue. They walk directly between the British regiments at Cliveden and the American cannons in front of Upsala, the 1795 Federal-style house across the way. Gathered behind ropes strung from tree to tree, the onlookers are strategizing as much as the soldiers as they jockey for the best position to see the battle. A man assures a boy in the crowd: *Don't worry they just use powder, not real rounds and you know what? At your age, you'd be old enough to be a soldier.* Back toward the house, a girl with a small boy on her shoulders comments that the leather flint covers were not really used at the time of the actual battle. This nineteen-year-old blond has been participating in reenactments since she was eight years old. She is a member of the Fifth Pennsylvania Regiment, reporting to battle and camping out in canvas tents, following strict military rules.

At Cliveden the British wait for a shot at the Americans. The canons fire, making a guttural thud. Car alarms on Morton Street stir, competing with the bagpipes. Canon smoke plays the role of the fog that actually enveloped Washington's troops and the autumn light adds to the surreal effect.

The Americans approach through a stand of hemlocks. A brutal gun battle commences. Soldiers advance, drop to the dirt, and fire back. The Red Coats, muskets pointing out the windows, fell the rebels one by one. A couple of Americans stagger by, flags in hand, pretending to bash down the front door. The enactment is so real, the visual symbols so rich and accurate, the sounds so brutal, that the caretaker of the house, standing with the spectators, flinches. Sometimes, perhaps, these soldiers go too far.

In thirty minutes the Americans are finished. The dead rise for lunch. They will do the whole thing again in a couple of hours, indifferent to the rest of Germantown, without the interest of most of Germantown, just obscene noise and no parking, an immutable event, always.

Barbara Cooper knew all this. She and her husband own Slim Cooper's, the jazz club her father-in-law started at Johnson and Stenton, ten blocks from Cliveden. The National Trust hired Barbara to reach out to the African American community in Germantown, to attempt to make them feel welcome, to tear down walls of resentment and indifference. Her steps have been careful and strategic. The improvements are the result of her relationships in the community. The black business owners who have been ignored by Cliveden for years were skeptical of the initiative, but several have participated in Barbara's events. She held an art show and a summer jazz festival that drew a few hundred neighbors and their lawn chairs. She rents the grounds and the carriage house for social events. The neighbors appreciate Barbara and her enthusiasm for the historical site. When she discusses slavery at Cliveden or Richard Allen, a former slave of Benjamin Chew who became the founder of the black Methodist church, during her talks about African American life at Cliveden, heads turn.

But real change takes time and Cliveden still keeps outsiders at arms length. Organizers of the Battle of Germantown advertise in the *Chestnut Hill Local* and in neighboring suburban papers, but not in the *Mount Airy Times-Express* or the *Germantown Courier*. Day to day historical interpretation does not include lessons on slavery or black life at the site, and most of the students who come on class trips are from private schools in the suburbs. As long as this is the case, a part of Germantown, a part of their own Gold Coast, remains off limits, effectively untouchable.

*

Above the roof of the farmer's market on Germantown Avenue, the billboard reads *McDonald's Means More*. The farmer's market is in a nondescript building next to the vacant Town Hall, a 1923 classical revival with curving sandstone walls and a staircase that's now covered with broken glass and careless filth. No one sits here to enjoy a sunny afternoon and watch the passersby on the avenue, let alone a pleasurable cigarette.

The sign above the entranceway to the market is Amish-fashioned—black and white with no frills. Below the de rigueur horse and buggy, it says the market is open Tuesday and Friday. The market is busy midday. Elderly black ladies line up for poultry. The butcher offers one woman a choice of two chickens. The old wood floors are bloodstained and beaten, the air yellow and unfiltered. Amish girls in hats and loquacious white-bearded farmers man the stalls. They sell peach cobbler, barbecue chicken, white loaves, and whiting filleted and prepared.

A black girl in a white uniform behind the counter at Newman's Grill asks a customer, *How you doin' today?* And he responds, *Real good especially when I am looking at you* and she, *That's what I like to hear.* A large white coconut cake sits on Newman's counter—the inside is yellow, like an egg yolk. Behind the counter they bend over backwards to be friendly. The stools are filled with regulars: laborers, men in suits and Burberries, men in fedora hats. Nurses and teachers come by for gumbo. The lemonade is fresh. A copy of the *Daily News* is always available, *Counter Copy* written in Sharpee, to go with chicken salad and fries. The farmer's market is comfortable like this, easy and essential. It is as saturated with the everyday lives of middle-class African Americans as it is with unprocessed meat, with butchering scents and fried dough.

Things have changed on Germantown Avenue where Essie used to shop from midcentury until her death. The farmer's market would be familiar as would the bench in Vernon Park. Otherwise, if Essie were to walk the avenue today, she would stand on the corner confused. On the corner of Germantown and Chelten, Allen's variety and Rowell's Department Store are gone as are the J.C. Penney and the Orpheum Theatre. Even Asher's candy couldn't stay.

The shoppers are overwhelmingly black. This alone might surprise her. The sidewalk is crowded. Discount chains with bright florescent aisles and ghetto shops have replaced the old stores. The avenue reports a street poetry. It blares. It is corrupt and hot. Vendors hawk videotapes and oils. Stores sport bright colored sweatshop clothes. Their names pronounce the firmament: Remy's Paradise Florist, Most Pleasant Memories, Sassy Beauty Outlet, Fatah's African Braiding, Tropicor Lounge, Golden Bell Clothing, Fantastic Finishes Hair Salon, Susan's Wigs, Shape 'n Style, Barron's for Men, Shirley's for Kids, Funcoland, Fadbulous, Pizza Pazzi.

Where Essie would have stood to wait for the trolley home, she would now see a line form for lottery tickets at the newsstand. She would be greeted by music from Top Flight, the clothing store. She would hear a belligerent man arguing with his contractor on a cell phone, *the windows should have been in ten to twelve weeks ago*. She might pick up a newspaper and read a story like this one in the Inquirer: "a Germantown man was shot and killed in his car in an apparent ambush attack just before 2:30 A.M. Saturday, police said. Harold Miller, 23, of Manheim Street near Germantown Avenue, was parked a block from his home, at Manheim and Wade streets, when he was shot three times in the chest, police said. Police said that, so far, they don't know why Miller was shot or who might have done it." Essie would find traces of her neighborhood—and so much more. Did Essie's Gold Coast ever exist? Was it part of the bedrock beneath her feet? Or was it merely something that existed in the community's collective heart, a purely ephemeral possession?

7. THE STREET

THE slate sidewalk on Second Street slopes to the curb. It is disfigured by cracks and weeds. Late on a bright day, the sun reflects hard against the row of buildings across the street—everything is butterscotch yellow. And generally but for the wind it is quiet.

Fins and Swedes temporarily claimed this Delaware riverfront as part of New Sweden in 1630. What was then swampy open humid meadow—home to muskrat, beaver, ancient sturgeon, wild turkey, and deer—is now a cluster of winding streets. Small bands of Lenni Lenape indians trapped, hunted, and fished here. Only after William Penn paid one thousand pounds to the Lenapes in 1682, did the marsh reeds and dense woodland, the endless, saturated stands of oak, hickory, chestnut, and elm begin to disappear.

From the front of a clothing store and across the low macadam corner, the old street languishes, distorted and incomprehensibly ugly. Its width suggests a wild west set more than something out of early English colonial America. We find clues to its market past: dormer windows and pitched roofs, wide glass storefronts and inset doorways of patterned ceramic tile, double garage doors, fancy cornices with carved bows and flowers, and urnlike crowns reaching to the low sky, stretching this ordinary row-house world to the heavens above.

By 1830, with thirty thousand pioneers residing in wood and brick row houses, the Northern Liberties district was considered the seventh largest city in the nation. It was harder and freer than neighboring Philadelphia. The street vibrated with metal carriage wheels sharply grinding the fine dirt road. On Second Street, where they built an open-air marketplace, voices of gypsies and hucksters competed with the sounds of sea gulls swirling above. Goats and chickens wandered between the buildings.

Now, listless and bitten tracts of land constitute the once-booming market town. The landscape is delirious and difficult to digest. Several abandoned cobblestone alleys surround Second Street along with a hemlock forest, lawn furniture, and cluttered patches of tomato plants. All within a few city blocks is a blurry snapshot of a place in motion, locked in a moment of time. Here are two abandoned breweries, a brew pub, and a jazz house. Amidst two-and-half-story brick row houses and chestnut-covered industrial alleys are a poultry processor, a Russian, a Ukrainian, and a Greek Orthodox church, stables and grazing fields for the city's tourist carriage industry, and countless gardens. A tannery has been turned into a neighborhood park. In this tangle are two automotive brake reliners—one clean the other a neighborhood nuisance, a Greyhound depot, an ecstasy dance club, and a titty bar where an obsession with a dancer named Summer caused a suburban swindler to kill his wife. Just around the corner from a city councilman's Caribbean villa are live-work loft condominiums for artists. And sharing this same spot are an eighteenth-century church that houses a greasy fence manufacturer, a vending cart factory, the bones of the first Catholic bishop in America, and a Kosher bakery that specializes in challah.

Second Street is a collision of dreams. One after the other, each dream has changed the street. The Lenapes dreamed of stars and trout, the first British colonists of money. Welsh and German immigrants dreamed of work. The Jews that followed from Germany dreamed of stature and acceptance. African Americans dreamed of peace, artists of space and low rent. The street itself keeps every dream alive. Centuries of human lives are trapped in Second Street's asphalt, in the cobblestone and wood below, in slate and granite that line the way. These lives constitute a living force that guides the hands of those on the street today. Past dreams are still lingering. They never let go.

Yet none take hold. No one—not the mighty Indians whose land this was for centuries, nor the fierce, hardscrabble immigrants, the entrepreneurial Jews, the insistent and committed artists—governs the street, not for long. At any moment, the street represents a newly concocted jumble of dreams. It changes endlessly, in ways no one can control, certainly in ways no one can predict.

We spy on Second Street at the beginning of the twenty-first century. The air is filled with expectation: at last, the papers say, the neighborhood is arriving. For thirty years, this has been Philadelphia's "next" neighborhood, about to happen. Even as I write them in jest, to make a point, these words sound shrill and empty. Second Street has been "happening" for centuries—pulsing, gushing with real human dreams. The street itself is covered in scars, the result of constant, unrelenting tumult. We need only to watch for a short time to witness dreams colliding, to see the street itself change, to see a building stand, then fall, and to smell the dust that bellows in its place.

It has been twenty-five years since Frank Hyder and Ira Upin moved to Second Street. Some say that Frank and Ira were the first ones in, frontiersmen. Such a statement is ridiculous of course. Several thousand people lived in the neighborhood at the time they arrived. Hundreds of families had recently settled on the western edge of the Northern Liberties. Many on George and Lawrence and Olive and Cambridge had never left.

But Second Street seemed then like a ghost town. The open-air Jewish market that came to dominate the blocks between Spring Garden and Brown was closed in 1960. The market shed that covered the middle of the street had been torn down. Of the once-prosperous German Jewish community that surrounded the market, only Sonny Rosenberg and Mickey Grossman and Harry Shur were left. The three men held on to Second Street, still playing out their own dreams, still grasping, still breathing. Rosenberg's dream was really a nightmare, as a neighbor puts it. He grew up on Green Street, a few blocks from the wealthy and status-conscious community on Second. He dated a rich girl from Second Street who spurned his love when she realized his family was not wealthy enough. He never got over it. When Frank and Ira arrived on the street in the midseventies, Sonny was taking revenge by purchasing old mansions and allowing them to deteriorate. Once he encouraged the city to demolish an historic house even though a couple was ready to purchase and renovate it. His dream was to erase the very last vestige of the girl and her contemptuous world.

Mickey Grossman was serving sickening slop, which he called the Trashman's Special, at his bar. The Trashman's Special made Frank ill the first time he tried it. And Harry Shur, cursing and berating his hardware store customers, was slowly going insane. As dusk settled on any given evening in the midseventies on Second Street, an eerie quiet took over. Then Johnny Babbick, dirty and disheveled, whose two houses were so full of collected junk that he had to clear an eighteen-inch trail just to move around, would make his way to the street. Mr. Big Balls, suffering from elephantiasis of the testicles, was there too. His terrible stench, the puss-reek of a man living without plumbing, would drive everyone else away.

But Frank and Ira came. They came to Second Street to find cheap space and comfort. Frank paid $8,500 in cash for a six-thousand-square-foot house built in 1820 that had been vacant for forty-five years. With the cash, the seller of the house bought a new 1976 Buick. In and around this house, Frank Hyder has created a dream world, a place to paint and live, to grow, and raise six children. Frank had been living in the neighborhood for a year when Ira Upin moved to American Street, right behind the west side of

Second. And there, the painters, one on each side of the wide, ugly street, forged a new place with new layers of life on top of, but also absorbed by, the street and its lingering past.

When Frank bought his house—a house with eight fireplaces, the one-time house of the founder of the New Yorker Cheese Company, a house with original milk paint on the trim—he had never built anything or given a thought to home repair. He turned to do-it-yourself books from the Free Library. When he was in want of materials, Frank took off on his bike across the city, where he found everything he needed. It was all there—monstrously cumbersome 150-pound beams, floor tile, woodwork, thousands and thousands of bricks in massive piles, the heaping remnant of someone's house reduced to rubble. For the rest, he stuck closer to home. Harry Shur advanced him the remaining materials he needed.

When Frank met Harry Shur, he was still known as the King of Nails. This short, wiry man hauled leaden boxes of nails on his shoulder from one storage location in one building to a warehouse in another. His four-story, nineteenth-century mercantile buildings were stockpiled with fourteen million pieces of hardware. At the height of his business, to have stopped in the store, even for a single item, meant a long wait as Harry took care of his regular customers, the city's independent hardware store owners. These old-fashioned men would follow him around the store like devoted religious disciples as he searched dusty shelves and moldy browned boxes for two-and-a-quarter-inch cut masonry nails or screen door latch springs.

Harry Shur was a decent, intense man. He worked every day of the year. On Christmas, as Harry stood alone outside his store, Frank Hyder would come over to talk and keep him company. That is how the painter with a bushy salmon-colored beard and fish-tank green eyes and the curious hardware man became friends. They traded stories. Or more likely Frank listened to Harry. While Harry may not have realized he was losing his mind, Frank did. As the hardware industry changed and demographics shifted, Harry held on blindly. Though he still handed out cash when a child was born in the neighborhood, he was no longer considered a friendly fixture but a neighborhood nuisance. Frank knew that Harry, with his ten decrepit buildings, was in part responsible for the sorry state of the street. He watched his friend become belligerent and offensive. Shur would not sell his buildings despite the countless fines and violations and the myriad offers to purchase them. His disheveled pigtail-wearing arthritic sister Lena by his side, Harry would not leave Second Street. He said it over and over. *They will have to take me away.*

At that time, stories about Harry Shur reverberated around Second Street, careening off the concrete base of Interstate 95, settling all around. The *Daily News*, the local newspaper known for its thorough neighborhood beat, picked up on Harry and his derelict properties, his stupefying hardheadedness in the face of all kinds of opposition. When Harry was finally taken to a nursing home and his power of attorney placed in the hands of a nephew, the paper reported that Harry "dressed in a shabby manner and kept his properties just as shabby." Ron Avery, the reporter on the scene, envisioned Harry's properties "rising from the rubble, infusing Northern Liberties with new hope and enthusiasm."

Ira Upin came to Second Street from Skokie, Illinois. The flat, drawn sound of his voice betrays his Midwestern upbringing. He came east to be a painter. He paints massive canvases that hang front to back in his cluttered second-floor studio. He makes bold conceptual art that matches his personality—bright, direct, and engaging. There is a nuclear mushroom cloud, the word *idea* painted onto canvas, and a series on the four senses. The paintings of the senses are Ira's most graphic and aesthetically accessible.

For Ira Upin it seems life is measured in decades rather than years. In his first decade in the Northern Liberties, Ira had created his own world. He renovated factories and houses. He painted huge canvases. His daughter grew older. Ira struggled with cancer. Seeking space, he eyed an empty two-story warehouse behind his house, which, if torn down, would provide him with an ample yard. The building's owner refused to sell. Meanwhile, his neighborhood boomed and then busted a few years later. Neighbors worked together and separated.

As Ira waited for the owner of the warehouse to change his mind, across Second Street Frank became worried. The city had just demolished the historic house next door because the owner owed merely $265 in school taxes. Ray Biddle, the real estate man two doors down, bought the lot and a little house behind it. Frank feared that Ray would sell his own building, the small house, and the lot to an industrial business or a warehouse. With young children, he didn't want an invasive industrial outfit right next door. Eventually, with the little cash he had saved, he bought the lot himself and the small house in the back. He fenced the lot and turned the house into a studio, the studio where Frank Hyder would meld conceptual and figurative art in a dark and mystical way.

After a while, Frank's paintings received recognition. On a National Endowment for the Arts fellowship, he traveled to Peru, Colombia, and Turkey. He taught in Caracas. He learned ancient meanings, adapted materials. Frank found his themes, discovered the historical tension, the native-colonial grip, the play for the land, the fragile culture. Back in Philadelphia, one night he and his wife woke to find a police officer in their bedroom. The front door was wide open, and paintings and materials were gone. The burglars had come in through the empty lot, entered the house on the side, and walked out the front door. Frank felt exposed and violated. He became determined to guard himself, protect his family, his work, and his life. But instead of simply constructing a wall across the lot, Frank took a month and built a single-story structure, a new studio.

Frank Hyder is as boyish and eager as Ira Upin is patient and strong willed. Frank had become enchanted with the hidden court-yards of South America, the lush tile-covered, orange-scented spaces. Secret, but common, social places. With his new studio en-closing the yard, the fifty-foot-high wall of Interstate 95 and the tracks of the Elevated train serving as the east portico, Frank Hyder built a Philadelphia courtyard of brick and foundation stone. He constructed balconies, carved a pond, grew saplings taken from the park in soil he dug out of the river's edge a few blocks a way. He planted Austrian grapevines, built a two-story storage shed, a makeshift garage, and a bridge across the pond where cats lean over and curr at the fish.

Eventually Frank cleaned out his original studio and found a tenant, a guitar-maker, to fill the space. Chris DiPinto has played guitar since he was five years old. His hair kept in a ponytail with red elastic, Chris mumbles softly as if he is speaking to himself. He builds guitars and sells vintage electrics from the sixties and seven-ties and used amplifiers. Chris and Sophie DiPinto came from Market Street in neighboring Old City. In three years there, Chris and Sophie witnessed Market Street change. They watched, mes-merized, as a dollar store became an expensive restaurant, and they wondered where the musicians had gone. Several of the clubs closed. More than a few local indie rock bands broke up and DiPinto Guitars was caught with fewer customers in a drifting local scene. When their rent was increased by 300 percent, they too were chased out of Old City. Now, colorful, futuristic guitars cover the walls of Frank Hyder's old studio on Second Street.

On the corner where Harry and his brother opened the hardware store in 1935, the 700 Club opened in 1997, providing neighborhood artists with a place to gather over beer. John the bartender, a pip-efitter, whose face is red and round—a face of another time— or-chestrates monthly nights of opera, where he plays famous recordings in the bar. Otherwise the bar is the center of a trendy but artist-infused social scene, and the Liberties, a youthful playground, is becoming cool.

On a cold night in January, a block and a half from Shur's old empire and two from the 700 Club, William Reed stands behind the bar he hand built, wiping down the fifty-year-old stainless taps he found down the street at the architectural exchange. A 1940s GE refrigerator is tapped, ready to serve the coldest beer of the house, Yuengling Chesterfield Ale. Made by the oldest brewery in the nation, and often served as a bar's first-rate offering, here at the Standard Tap it is the cheapest beer served. Will is training a new waiter, methodically filling a small glass with the house beers, each of which is made locally and served from a tap. The new waiter smiles at the last of the beers, a rich, complex Stoudt's. It is brown and dense, like a bar of gooey rum shaving soap. The tavern's original tin ceiling is painted a thick shiny black. The place is dark and comfortable.

When Will and Liz and four-year-old Nora moved into the third and fourth floor of the old Bullshead Inn—a British lookout during the Revolutionary War and the site of the first railroad demonstration in the nation—they had no cash, but they became instant local heroes. The last owner had left the place with bad debt and lingering anger. They renovated the inn themselves as they had the cash and time. Three years later they opened the doors to a neighborhood that was becoming a street in transition and upheaval, a place unfurling.

*

Ira's retreat is a minimalist garden, a small patch of bright green lawn, a few flowers, some lettuce, and basil. The thick spicy odor of late summer marigolds fills the muggy air. A space like this is not unusual in the oldest parts of the city that stretch along the banks of the Delaware. Nearly every row house was afforded some exterior space for a privy, a few chickens, a place to grow herbs. Thick walls, built and rebuilt from brick and stucco and cinder block, divide these tiny odd-sized, often chilly moss-covered sanctuaries.

Ira's rectangular preserve reaches far from the back of American Street to the rear of Second. It is unusually spacious and open, resulting not from the compassion of the eighteenth-century builders who created the brick settlement, but from the passing of time and people. As density has fallen, so have many buildings. Bright warm early morning light filters across the flat New Jersey pinelands from the Atlantic Ocean. The pink light covers the unrepentant sprawl of South Jersey, illuminating the swimming pool-blue Ben Franklin Bridge at the southern base of the Northern Liberties. Luck and stubbornness gave Ira Upin some of this morning light. The owner of the warehouse finally relented. In the end, as if patience was the simple price to pay for more room, he handed the property to the painter. So the brick and rubble backfill of the demolished warehouse has become Ira's earth where his geometrical lawn grows today. The eastern light from the Pinelands wilderness reaches the garden through a literal hole in the fabric of Second Street. The hole, really a grim gravel parking lot, was created by the demolition of a few of Harry Shur's neglected buildings.

The sun rises way above the chain-link fence surrounding the lot and into the painter's yard. He sits in this unadorned patch, with the remains of Harry Shur's windowless and decrepit real estate all around. But some of that real estate is now his. Ira bought two of Harry's buildings to convert into four apartments and a restaurant. For more than twenty years, Ira has worked construction jobs in the summer in order to paint in the winter. He bought and renovated a few other buildings himself, including the New Yorker Cheese factory that surrounds Frank's house. The construction work allowed him to do nothing but paint for an entire decade.

He and Frank individually, and also together, have forever altered the material corps but also the essence of Second Street. Shur is gone, though many of his buildings still stand in his worn place, and Grossman too. Sonny Rosenberg remains along with his lingering hatred for the street. Artists and furniture designers, guitar makers and brewers have come over time. They surround Second Street. Now the neighborhood is the greatest artists' colony in the state. These newer residents, too, have fixed up the old buildings, displaying pottery and sculpture in old storefront windows.

Ira Upin thinks often about his changing neighborhood. He knows well that he is living in a peculiar place, where almost anything is accepted, where he still finds neighbors living in corners he did not know existed. As he builds luxury apartments and a restaurant where a grungy old man once peddled nails, Ira wonders if the neighborhood wasn't a little more special a decade ago, so bizarre a place that it was easy and comfortable to fit in. He feels queasy, a dark ambivalence to this place he himself has partially created, a place in continuous flux and unremitting metamorphosis.

*

The shop owner stands toward the back of his store. Late in the autumn afternoon, a Thanksgiving darkness approaching, it is deceptively bright in the gray, white, and black room. After almost a year, he is used to the quiet hours. He had chosen this location to craft the business at a steady pace, methodically, like a photograph to be perfectly exposed and developed.

Sebastian Charles Porter McCall moves gently, without sound, to the front of the store in the center near the shoe display. He peers out through the restored storefront window, beyond the words *Charles Porter Boutique* scripted in gold. He waves as someone familiar passes by. He has lived in this neighborhood all his life. He glances down and checks a message on his beeper and thinks about life as an entrepreneur. As much as he plans and learns from others, he never knows where he will end up. So he chose, at the age of twenty-five, to start in a place he already knew.

Sebastian McCall's features are fine. His mocha skin is clear. His eyes meet the world wide open. He is tall. He dresses well in strong colors and speaks softly but confidently. He thrives on human contact, but prefers genuine one-on-one connections. He can do without the overbearing pulse of the crowd. So he barely tolerates the weekly buying trips to New York.

Standing motionless at the front of his store at Second and Brown, he remembers his mother's struggle to start her own hair salon and his parents' agony and rage and failure. But the McCall Beauty Salon became a part of the fabric of the Northern Liberties, a local business and a gathering place. He envisions his mother there, in the back room, and he imagines Mrs. Santos or another neighbor in the chair. His mother fits the woman with a hairpiece. Grandchildren chase after one another as neighbors stop by to chat or pass the time until dinner.

The stillness of Sebastian's empty store is punctured only by the sound of a megaphone on top of a passing car. *Vote for John Street. Vote for John Street for mayor!* He pictures his mother's salon as it was when he was a teen, before his son Pierre was born, before his first business cleaning carpets. The salon harbored all of them, held the family and the block together. Still, he feels the icy scream of teenage pregnancy and plans dismantled. He sees himself at eighteen, scrambling to find an apartment, start a new business, and care for a child. The Northern Liberties kept him centered and focused his energy. He found an apartment at American and Poplar, a block from this store. He saw Rosaura Hernandez then. He noticed her right away but she was young, too young, and untouchable. When he saw her again she was off to college. At that time, he was starting his second business, selling handbags and accessories in his mother's hair salon, product marketing to a captive audience.

To learn retailing, Sebastian took a job at the Shirt Corner in Old City. Shirt Corner and its cousin, Suit and Tie Corner, are the loud relatives no one wants to see at family gatherings. They embarrass everyone. And here they are, both (the owners, brothers, do not speak—a squabble over the family inheritance) in the middle of historic Philadelphia, a block from Benjamin Franklin's house, two from the Liberty Bell, and they are dressed up for the occasion. The stores are painted bright red, white, and blue with stripes but no stars. Their windows are filled with chartreuse suits, alligator shoes, white fedora hats. But there Sebastian learned the business, waiting on church pastors and reverend. From the store window, he watched Rosaura waiting for the bus at Third and Market. Later, when he was not driving to the suburbs to see her at college or selling handbags or manning the floor at Shirt Corner, Sebastian was planning his own store. Like most entrepreneurs, Sebastian envisioned the world he would create, pictured it clearly in his mind.

Later, when Rosaura took him to the sea, the perfect, illuminated, green and blue milk of the Caribbean, he was afraid to take a swim. It had never occurred to him to learn. For a neighborhood boy whose mother owned her own business, there was no time to cross into Jersey and go down to the shore. He never had time to think of waves and hard hot sand and the salty taste of the sea. The farthest he had been from the McCall Beauty Salon at Fifth and Poplar was to visit his father's family in South Carolina. But after a while he stopped going on those unbearable, smoke-filled, sticky-vinyl-seat trips.

When Sebastian was ready to open his own store, he searched for a location. The entrepreneur knew many people in Old City, and he recognized that it was trendy and rich. Lawyers and advertising executives had long since driven most of the artists from the converted factories and Market Street was full of crowded restaurants and late nineties stock market euphoria. But he didn't feel comfortable there.

He opened the Charles Porter boutique at Second and Brown, three blocks from his childhood home, in early December with only the merchandise he could afford. He added menswear and women's shoes later. He bought them with his personal credit card. Rent was cheap enough for him to take his time, learn in a relatively quiet environment, test some ideas.

Almost a year in and Sebastian was seeing an average of five customers a day, just enough to break even. At first he was content with a few regulars, and he expanded his line. In quiet hours, Sebastian watched the street changing. He watched the Standard Tap being finished, Ira Upin renovating Harry Shur's buildings, and live-work lofts being built across the street. He watched the coffee shop open then close. His customers said they liked the location. He loved the Northern Liberties. It was his nest. But he did not start the business for the neighborhood. Five customers a day were not enough. On a warm night he and Rosaura drove ten blocks south to Old City, where the sidewalks were filled with his customers. He returned the next day and noticed a storefront under construction. He found the owner and signed a lease. A week later Charles Porter was open on Market Street. At Second and Brown a heavy black gate still hides Sebastian's scripted gold sign.

8. THE BARRIO

THE Broad Street subway sounds a subterranean bellow. Like a heaving stomach, the bursts of noise come and go sometime before the train haltingly approaches the station. Willful fluorescent light braises the ratty tile in the station. The air outside is as crisp as a washed up claw under a sandal-clad foot, but the cool air does not reach down below. The air in the station is hot, unbearable. At eight in the morning the station is noticeably empty. The wide orange car is full, a sleepy mass of ties, dress shoes, overcoats, and khakis. The full-color quick-fact *Metro* tabloid spreads its paper wings in half the hands. A man in thick bifocals *davens* while holding five copies. The car stops at City Hall, where the city's two subway lines intersect and all the trolley lines converge. Bank workers, gray lawyers, and corporate accountants transfer to the trolley in a racing squirm. A greasy flower man sits on a wooden bench. A man with a red and white plastic pushcart careens on, *Inquirer, Daily News!* As if no one in the tunnel knows the names of the city's two dailies. Nurses in pink, purple, and green scrubs keep their heads down while heading up the stairs to the El, going west.

The subway car shakes and rolls through the tunnel. The doors shuffle open and thin, stylish university students fill the flat industrial orange seats. A Chinese film student wearing wine-colored lipstick sits facing front next to a window as the local moves at half speed to Race-Vine. Only occasionally does the subway man call out the stops. Elegant baby blue, hunter green, burgundy, and navy tile typeset along the station walls is all that reminds us of rich industrial North Philly. The old station names shine amidst brightly lit ghetto grime, poster ads, and hazy bullet proof glass. After the students leave the train, the car feels cavernous. A tall man in dreadlocks, a ponytail, and clunky black shoes, reads a worn leather bible. Above him a sign says, *Have you been raped, attacked, injured or had other traumas?*

The express train blows past, a creamsicle blur. A twenty-year-old mother, whose hair is close cropped and bleached, and her four-year-old son, blue robot toys in each hand, enter. They find what must be customary seats at the front of the car facing north, she in the first, he behind. She bites her nails, and as the train stops, the boy stands before the doors, waiting. *Open it, open it!* He shouts during the laborious pause, an empty vigil, and then, *ping! ping!* They go out into the cigarette-stained station.

Outside, the day is moving slowly. The air warms and thickens. Latin music comes in waves, from cars stopped at the corner, from groupie station wagons, from girlfriends' radios. The graffiti writers compare colors. They share paint as their names take shape. The *psst, psst, psst* of the cans is endless. Hands to the wall, their work is addictive and forceful.

The writers complete the black background first. Danny is now outlining his name in a green the color of glacial water. Joe, who is still, quiet, and drunk from the night before, is just getting started. His sketch sits on the sidewalk between his feet. Tom has already finished his tag. His lines are aggressive and thin. Orange milk crates jammed with spray cans fill the back seats of their cars and the sidewalk. The writers pace themselves, talk, and ask advice. One by one, they step back from the wall, smoke, and piss around the corner.

Spray paint blows west then east and then disappears, but the cancer-odor remains and saturates the bright air. We notice scribbling on the sidewalk and telephone poles in teal and blue, gray, brown, silver, fuchsia, and chartreuse. The scribbles appear to be the work of amateurs. But scribbles, every writer must remember, represent the origins of their art, the earliest tags on the New York subway, quick and punchy motion.

The writers finish the wall in one day. It is seasonally themed for Halloween: ghosts and goblins, headless horsemen and all. A legal wall is a charm. The project is a thank you to the neighbors in the Barrio, a gift in return for acceptance. Nowhere else do neighbors appreciate, even welcome, the writer's art. Here, they can work in the open, in the light of day. Already they have come together to transform other walls with their intricate and raw writing, with their symbolic form. The last theme was outer space. With spaceships and planets the writers created a visual and symbolic departure from their daily lives, from the weeds that sprout between cracks in the sidewalk and the flattened beer cans that clutter the edges of their world.

Across Cecil B. Moore Avenue, smoke rises above a chain-link fence. The coarse smell of burning wood intercepts the odor of the paint. Ash particles swirl black and red against the blue sky. A forklift operator moves wooden pallets from one side of a lot to the other. Presumably these pallets too will burn. On the opposite corner of Fifth Street, a water spray reaches fifty feet, cooling falling brick and dampening the rubble and dirt of a demolition site. Not much more than the front façade of a nineteenth century mill remains. The mammoth building evaporates in the clash cry of overgrown machines. Despite the giant hose the corner fills with dust. The dust spreads out to the street. It mingles with the wood ash and the smoke, the paint mist and the sickening smell of toluene. Together the particles jumble in the air and fall steadily, like pesticide or fertilizer from a single-engine plane.

The row of mills continues up Fifth Street facing the Halloween wall. These are some of the city's handsomest old factories. Out front some of the artists that live and work inside watch the writers. Up above their heads, plants decorate an iron balcony. An orange notice is pasted to the door of the last of the mills, announcing the intent to build forty-five loft apartments.

On this day, this corner at the southern edge of the Barrio in Philadelphia, a half a block from the factory where 3,500 men and women once came together to turn the fur of rabbit, muskrat, and beaver into Stetson hats, is the fury of motion, of creation, of destruction. Human energy is deployed here in concentrated bursts. People react and interact and act on this environment. It moves in all directions.

Only at night when the spray-painted full moon above the headless horseman glows and the day's detritus settles to the ragged street below and car radios jostle the silence, only then is the motion hidden. The energy is draped in darkness and held tightly. In the morning light it shows. Tom's tag—*SEW*—his personal mark, has been tagged by another writer. Graffiti is still a competitive art form. It is a battle for space and a message. True to its origins, it is steady, ceaseless motion.

The city's body is like the writer's wall. The motion *is* ceaseless. Even in Philadelphia, a city with a deserved reputation for stasis and glacial, deal-breaking bureaucracy, the cityscape continues in an inexhaustible flux. I say flux because the process is not development. Development implies progress, moving ahead. Nor is the process gentrification. It is not a transformation.

When we measure the life of a street by the force of colliding dreams, Fifth and Cecil B. Moore registers a colossal explosion. This intersection reverberates. If someone were to ask, *what is it like there?* How would we reply? Would we say that it's burning, that it's the last vestige of the industrial city? Instead of building anything, they burn lousy wooden pallets. Would we say it's just another demolition site? They're clearing land there for redevelopment. Really? Aren't artists colonizing old factories? Haven't graffiti writers taken ownership of a trucking company's wall? Isn't it just another empty, dangerous corner in the Barrio? It is, of course, all these things.

Five blocks to the east, I climb the steps of the Elevated stop at Front Street. The horizon extends forever northeast out toward the river, and back into the jumbled city, into a field of Dominican bodegas and Colombian murals and symbolic graffiti. But none of those details are visible from the platform, not the hookers on Front Street or the produce store or the children playing soccer in the square beneath the cathedral. Instead, from here the city seems to be unbroken and homogenous: brick houses, brick factories, and churches. It looks like all of Philadelphia has looked for one hundred years.

The train cuts through the humid air. Through tinted windows, the brick mass is now a blur. Church steeples and factory smoke stacks, tall brown grass in someone's neglected lot, old stores that were built right against the tracks, empty banks, empty warehouses, out-of-date signs: all this is a rush of motion. The train drills past Kensington, roughly parallel to the river. It's surrounded by a great industrial amalgam, by rambling lives and cultures and fortune. Every few minutes the train stops, so too the city. I stare out the window. At last, here is the city *as it is*. A minute later the train pulls out of the station and the city is moving again. The city *as it is* was just an illusion.

*

Sara Ortiz, whose hair is strawberry blond and face is freckled, comes from Mayagüez, from the coast of Puerto Rico that faces the Dominican Republic. The night she flew to New York and then down to Philadelphia was cold. The trip seemed endless. It was February 1956, and she was nine years old. She came with her grandparents and her sister. Winter in Philadelphia—and here she was a child of the Caribbean. In Mayagüez she would go from house to house and always feel like she was at home. Here she felt like a car stuck on the ice, spinning its back wheels, spewing thick exhaust, and screeching a primal scream.

To Sara, the city was brutal and incomprehensible. She was stripped of her identity, thrown into a class taught only in English despite being filled with Spanish-speaking children. Only later, as an English-speaking adult, did she figure out what Ms. Schaeffer was saying. None of them understood then. They were caught between cultures: Americans but not really, *Boriquenos, Tainos, Caribs, Criollos, Indios, Africanos, Hispanicos*. She had been forced to leave her island. Her father, a union activist, was exiled from Puerto Rico for crying independence. He was exiled to the United States he had struggled against. Sara's parents never considered returning to the island. So she was trapped in a city that didn't fit her, in a family that had compromised itself just by boarding a plane.

Sara is outgoing and strong willed and in possession of a bright and relentless smile. With these qualities, she found a place in Philadelphia; her sister did not. Refusing to speak in school, she was demoted from fourth grade to kindergarten and still today she speaks only Spanish. For Sara it was easier to assimilate but everyday she struggles too.

Within a few years of arriving in Philadelphia, Puerto Ricans were pushed out of a neighborhood called Spring Garden and out across Broad Street to Kensington. Sara's parents settled there in 1956, near Norris Square, a wide, tree-filled park with factories all around. Though they were becoming unfashionable, Stetson hats were still made at Fourth Street, three blocks away from her house.

Sara struggled through school. *She has a learning disability*, the teachers and principals said, though Sara knew it was the language holding her back. She married at nineteen. She and her husband moved to Fifth and Diamond in the heart of a place that was fast becoming the Barrio. They moved north with their people, though her husband wanted to assimilate and to forget the Puerto Rico of his past. The stores had signs in Spanish and within a short time the business community named Fifth Street for the prize of the *conquistadores*. They called it *El bloque de oro*. Green and blue and gold waves, a sign of Caribbean warmth, were painted on the sidewalk.

Sara Ortiz has lived in Philadelphia for more than forty-five years. Her husband and children are fully assimilated. She is not. Though she is a leader in Philadelphia's Barrio, she does not feel comfortable here. This is not her city. When Sara thinks about the Barrio, she envisions her own struggle to maintain and celebrate Puerto Rican culture while claiming a spot in a cold and foreign place. How do we settle on ground that is always shifting beneath our feet?

Puerto Rican immigrants are especially mobile. They still come from the island. Some two hundred thousand Puerto Ricans have come to Philadelphia. Some stay. Others go back and forth, visiting relatives, chasing seasonal work, for vacation. It drives teachers and librarians crazy. Sara, too, is on the chase, union organizing in Puerto Rico part of the year, following the steps of her father, following the tracks to what she still calls home.

And on the flight north, she and many others cling to the visions of gentle hills, brown fields, and thick humid air. And the breeze. Their dreams are lived out in the Barrio, where a man raises goats on red dirt that once supported tall town houses, mansionettes for factory managers. Down the block where a bulldozer has exposed still more earth, where children crowd the stoops of the few remaining buildings and others circle the sidewalk on bicycles, brown-skinned men pass summer days at a wooden roadside stand painted purple. They sit at tables amidst the rubble. The only palm trees are in murals painted on the walls. But Sara thinks her dreams have no place Philadelphia.

Gardens line Palethorp Street on the other side of the square from Sara's first house in Philadelphia. We find peppers growing in November, careful raised beds of tomatoes, benches, a pink work shed built to replicate a 1950's Puerto Rican bungalow, something like Sara's own house looked in Mayagüez. At Palethorp and Cumberland faded sunflowers cover a field next to a dense garden that someone decorated with carousel horses, old toilets, and lattice made from aluminum ladders. A giant painting of butterflies by the Cuban muralist Salvidor Gonzalez graces another garden. Farther north, flowers and vegetables grow on both sides of the street. Here, the view opens up. On the side of a building, someone has commissioned an early twentieth-century painting of farmers in the field, what appears to be the *Boriqueño* ideal.

A few blocks away on Front Street under the elevated tracks, the smell of fried fish drifts south. Vendors sell black baseball hats and play Caribbean music. There are four worn benches now hidden by weeds in a garden that once held someone's dream. Above, the elevated train stops. As if to mimic the fleeting, transient quality of the place, the recorded voice inside the train announces, *Doors are opening*, and then moments later, *Doors are closing*. Front Street vibrates slightly as the silver train pulls out of the station.

Sara Ortiz left this part of the Barrio when drug dealers burned the thick trees in Norris Square and tortured the children who tried to play there. She moved north again as thousands of working-class Puerto Ricans extended the Barrio up above the Boulevard, around the Church of the Incarnation. But this part of the Barrio, in an old neighborhood called Olney, was already filled with immigrant families from Portugal and Korea and the Middle East. The neighborhood is so diverse that the parish church offers Sunday mass in four languages, in services that stretch throughout the day. I join thousands of Catholics on a bright, frozen day in December, on the first Sunday of Advent. The *Iglesia Encarnación* is overwhelmed with people. Mass is given in English at nine in the upper cathedral. At 10:30 in the lower church, it is performed in Portuguese. Dark-haired people stream in from the neighborhood to attend mass in what is really the church basement. They are young families mostly, with many children. Altar boys carry a stark simple cross to the front as Friar José Nunes Dos Santos leads his followers. *Em nome do Pai, do Filho e do Espírito Santo.* Guitars strike a medieval chord and upstairs the cathedral fills with Latinos. After a priest gives announcements and masons in flannel shirts, young couples, and teenaged girls find seats, the whole of this fortress erupts in a song that floats to the apse and lingers in the air. *Tu eres palabra de Dios que revela su amor. Llena nuestro corazon de encendido fervor.* Mass is performed a second time in English at noon. Late in the afternoon, the day ends with a service in Creole. Then, the church basement opens to Haitians, but not until the last Dominicans have left.

They come to the Barrio now from other islands and continents. They are Dominican and Mexican, Cuban and Colombian, Venezuelan, Guatemalan. Every effort is made by these disparate people to work together as one Latino group, all the while celebrating each national and regional culture. At the *Iglesia Encarnación* all Latinos celebrate the Dominican *Virgen de la Altagracia* and independence in Nicaragua and Venezuela; Mexicans decorate the altar at Christmas.

Balancing cultural identities is a difficult, frustrating process. Some Puerto Ricans resent that other Latinos are benefiting from their own struggles. Others hope to build a Latino political consensus. They see the growth of the Barrio as an opportunity to increase power. All of them struggle to build American lives on top of other people's ruins.

Sara worries most about the children. Her compassion fills the cinderblock room in the school named for Roberto Clemente, the baseball hero of Puerto Rico and great humanitarian leader. She fought for this school, fought side-by-side with Johnny Irizarry, the school's *padrino*, to move it from the old hosiery factory where the elevators and the heat didn't work. Still she fights. She fights to install a crossing guard on Erie Avenue, traffic lights, and a walkway. She is fighting to stop neighborhood parties, the orgies that keep children out of school. She is fighting to keep away the gangs, the Latin Kings and Young Crazy Warriors, from Olney High and Edison. Sara Ortiz protects and honors her students. As a girl, she paid to go to school. She paid with her culture and language. They pay with bruises and with cash.

Sara's school is considered a success of sorts, and she is proud of the services and resources they offer to students and of the school itself, which is bright and colorful. Perhaps it is the Barrio's greatest monument, the single clearest statement of faith, of commitment, pronounced jointly by the community and the city. But as she sits in one of the new school's classrooms, she is drawn back to her own fourth grade experience. At one moment she was a carefree girl on a warm, rural island, and the next she was shivering, forced to adapt to someone else's language, someone else's rules, someone else's climate. She understands youthful ambivalence. She understands ambiguous identity. She understands what it is like to dream each night in Spanish, to dream of hot sun and shade, of open doors and fields and then to wake up inside the cold body of a city that is not her own.

*

Its front door hidden, the Roberto Clemente School is a maze surrounding a courtyard. Inside, signs in English exhort the students to do better. A dedication to the ballplayer and to the community is written in Spanish. A small woman guards the door. The art classroom, she says, is down the hall to the right, facing the courtyard.

Inside the room shades muffle the bright light reflecting off the snow. Immediately, I notice the familiar smell of art supplies: glue, paint, and pencil shavings. Stained glass panels made by the students hang near the windows. At the front of the room, eight of the students' portraits are taped to the wall. Giant paper birds and animals hang from string below the ceiling. It is oddly quiet as a class filled with mentally handicapped children winds down. A girl sponges a table and then at once all the students leave the room.

In the next class—fifth graders—they call their teacher, *Mister*. Wet snow falls in the courtyard outside the window and on the distant brick landscape—it's a scene with no middle ground. The children wear fluffy bright-colored coats to class as if they might walk into the cold at anytime. They want to wander—their energy is dispersed around the room—but the teacher wants them to focus on his demonstration of the finer points of papier mâché. He alternates criss-crossing batter-soaked layers of newspaper strips. *Don't leave air holes*, he reminds them. *Saturate means to soak every part of the newspaper with the flour and water.*

The class is self-segregated: girls at the long front tables, boys—all with closely shaven hair—in the back. Altogether they are evenly split Puerto Rican and African American. Altogether they box and slap each other, knock, crash into, and yell at each other. Some draw butterflies and bunnies, others dragons. A girl cries in frustration. Detentions are handed out like hot bills: one for you, one for you, one for you.

The teacher tries to continue the papier mâché demonstration but the students chatter incessantly.

—*Mister*
—*Mister*
—*Be quiet.*
—*Shut up so we can start.*
—*I know I sound white but . . .*
—*You are white.*

—*No I'm not. I'm black.*

—*You wish.*

—*I'm white. (Smile reveals a broken tooth.)*

—*I'm not white, I'm French.*

—*French.*

—*I only sound white because I lived with white people for ten years.*

—*Shut up.*

—*Be quiet.*

—*Shhh*

—*Mister, can we start?*

—*I won't talk over anybody.*

—*Shhh*

—*Be quiet.*

—*Shut up.*

—*Who are you? Why are you always here?*

—*I'm Puerto Rican.*

—*Mr. Popkin, what are you?*

—*Chinese.*

—*Chinese?*

—*Be quiet.*

—*Shut up.*

—*Can we start? I already know how to do this.*

—*No I don't talk over anybody.*

—*Mister, come on, it's quiet.*

—*Shut up.*

—*See, we are being quiet.*

—*Shhh*

—*Be quiet.*

—*Shut up.*

—*Mister, can I just start?*

—*No*

—*Hand me an apron.*

—*Shhh*
—*Be quiet.*
—*Shhh*

The entire hour melts like this. Outside the classroom window the snow diminishes in its intensity and small flakes blow against the building. The fifth graders move about the room, cleaning up what they had never really started. And their day goes on in fits and starts, one hour dissolving into the next. Eventually they are released to the bitten wind and gray streets. They dissolve into the streetscape—across the Barrio through the white, wet snow, the snow that wants to but cannot entirely muffle their uncertain identities.

9. THE INTERSECTION

JUST as the city keeps us inside its generous body, it also can push us away. Or worse, our relationship with the physical city can be one of ambivalence. Like the children who leave school only to dissolve into a barren, postindustrial landscape, we glide through the city, feeling neither push nor pull. We live as if in a loveless marriage.

In the fourth century of American city building, more and more of us are making marriage vows with the loveless city. We live in a landscape that is neither urban nor suburban. We live on old city streets that are injured by bad zoning, resulting in strip malls and careless parking lots, in what has become a confusing jumble, a city for cars. Living next to used car lots and muffler shops, our houses shake with passing trucks. We live on streets without public space, without street life. We wake up each morning on the fabled strip. But this is not the hot Las Vegas desert. It is the frozen, listless tundra of commercial real estate. Our dreams don't stick to the ice.

*

Olney Station is the last stop north on the Broad Street subway. Twelve bus lines intersect here amidst glass brick and bright signage. The station is new and user friendly. It is one of the busiest in the city, but its infrastructure can generally handle the crowds. At three o'clock in the afternoon it fills—every ledge, bench, corner, every inch of platform—with a multiracial, hormone-charged, adolescent mush. Girls High and Central High kids in their bright, tight fashions pose, waiting for a train, or not. When a train stops, the ambitious get on. The rest don't move, other than to continue talking.

Upstairs, Broad and Olney scrambles with still more students and women waiting for the bus and older women still, with shopping bags from downtown stores. Up a block or two, behind the Mr. C Famous Sweet Meat BBQ Beef-Chicken-Pork and across from four seven-story tudor apartment buildings, ten new houses are under construction. Broken glass, a hurricane bottle, a chicken wing, a crushed plastic Coke bottle, a mangled mint green pack of Newports cover the sidewalk on the sunny side behind a waiting bus. Here, the landscape is changing, caught in the in-between, torn by slack zoning, sixties modernist, low-slung, blank-walled mistakes, and careless building rules.

It is a thirty-minute trip from Norris Square in the Barrio to Broad and Olney, provided the wait isn't too long for the express train. Then transfer for the C bus to Sixty-sixth Avenue. For George Fillipello, who hates to drive, the bus and the subway are his connection to the world. George's bus flies up Broad Street, which is more like a small interstate here with six lanes including parking, passing a Korean funeral procession, two Chinese men talking, a teenage girl in a fluorescent white jacket, a high school sports star, a mother teaching her girls the times tables as they wait for the center city-bound bus in front of the Texaco station. Here, the street is tethered by a knockout competition between the fraying, traditional fabric of the pre-War city and the litter of the strip. Blows are exchanged, back and forth. The street is in constant flux. Only an allée of giant sycamores lends beauty, but the trees look foolish in front of strip malls, used car lots, and abandoned gas stations.

Motorists are well looked after on Broad Street. Surrounding a shopping center are ninety-five parking spaces and around them J's Auto, Marshall Auto Sales, Car Quest Auto Parts, and a host of used car dealers. *Like new!* the dealers announce: *One Owner, Low Mileage, Loaded.* The Amoco, Exxon, Thriftway supermarket, Speedy Muffler King, and Popeye's Chicken have each been abandoned.

A few blocks farther and George is home. He sits on the front porch of his house on Sixty-sixth Avenue and watches the street. A man down below the raised terrace talks about his pet cats and hopes for a cigarette, or twenty-five cents toward a loosie. It is early April. The air is thin and cold; the sun is warm.

George's red and yellow tulips are like a swell of Easter candy in his front yard. Bright green hosta, neatly measuring a foot apart, unswirl through broken soil. His grandmother's dwarf almond trees are in full bloom, the careful pink clusters too delicate for this scene. Later, after nights of warm rain, George's peonies and hyacinths and day lilies will appear.

George's acorn brown eyes are sad, at least they seem so. He has the tired, languid look of a religious disciple or a henchman in the Roman Empire. George rarely looks me in the eye. More often he stares down or out to the street where black girls in school uniform wait for the bus. George dresses in black: Lee jeans, cheap dress shoes, and a sweatshirt. He seems troubled—his is the countenance of a young gay man in the Catholic Church. George shares his childhood home with his ailing opera singer mother, gun-collecting city-cop sister, and with eight cats, a dog, and a cat cemetery under a sprawling fig tree—a descendent of a cutting his grandfather brought from Sicily in 1917. The front terrace garden has always been George's salvation and now with the 1920s house paint peeling, windowpanes missing, and wood trim rotting, it is his trophy and mission. Or it was until vandals destroyed the fishpond a couple of years ago.

George started building ponds and waterfalls around his house when he was fourteen. As a boy he watched the rainwater wash down the small front yard from the porch to the street. He was transfixed. George bought a water pump and created a cascade outside the back door of the house, down to the fig tree. Now water runs over terraced flagstones in the front of the house, down to the fishless pond that he rebuilt.

George loves old houses and architecture. In a grandmotherly tone, he calls his neighbors lovely. He calls his neighborhood a beautiful place to live. Only he wants desperately to get out, to find an old farmhouse far away from disrespectful kids, away from the unresponsive government, away from the drugs and danger he believes are lurking on the other side of Broad Street.

A bus stops again in front of the large corner twin next to George's house. The building houses offices built by a prominent African American physician and his sons, a dentist and a lawyer. Al Clark still practices dentistry there. He and his wife Della, an outspoken, high-energy visionary who broke her Texas high school's color line, live upstairs with their two kids. The elder Dr. Clark, who drove a Rolls Royce, made the place look regal, with white lions, a fountain, and a sunny atrium in glass.

Across the avenue stands a new drive-thru CVS/pharmacy, twenty feet from the curb line. Landscapers placed a large reddish rock, taken from a field in New Jersey or rural Pennsylvania, at the corner. George has seen the corner change twice in thirty years, from a Sunoco gas station to a Burger King, and now the pharmacy and its boulder. Beyond the CVS, a red and gray sign welcomes visitors to Team Dodge and offers penance to troubled buyers. *Bad Credit? You're Approved!*

Back across Broad Street is the Oak Lane Diner, a shiny stainless steel and chrome classic with a sign outside that says, *Welcome to Philadelphia.* Inside everything is burgundy and navy, black and white. It is smoky and busy all day, a black family hangout, where the chicken salad is dry and chunky, the old white waitresses gossipy and sweet. Deals go down here, and after-church pancakes and desserts swirl in a case. The diner sits on a triangular piece of prop-

erty in the middle of the intersection where Old York Road cuts between Broad Street and Sixty-sixth Avenue.

In a single breath while standing on his back steps, his five dead
cats buried just below him, George predicts that he will leave Sixty-
sixth Avenue in six months. He discusses plans for a greenhouse he
will build around the fig tree, the pruning schedule for the seventy-
year-old sycamore on the sidewalk in front of the house, the joy of
sitting on his front terrace at night, candles lit around him, watching the neighborhood. He realizes that he has been talking about
leaving for years, talking in circles. He wants to leave, but really he
is indifferent about the corner where he has lived all his life. The
brutal and inhuman landscape of CVS, the Dodge dealer, and the
Dunkin' Donuts is now so ordinary that George may not even realize he is being pushed away. He doesn't even know why his head
spins among the sycamore branches and neon signs. He simply
feels an urge to run, to seek shelter somewhere else. He stays because he loves to nurture his garden. He loves to tend his grandparents' trees. He loves to sit amidst his flowers.

He takes comfort in the sisters too, the nuns on Sixty-sixth
Avenue. He loves them. He buys their groceries. He minds their
walled garden. The stone Carmelite monastery was built in 1916 to
resemble an Umbrian country church with a thick red tile roof,
stone the color of brown fields, and village reserve. The church and
its walled forest of bright green trees cloisters eleven or twelve
Discalced Carmelite nuns, the spiritual descendants of St. Albert
Avogadro, who early in the thirteenth century gave the Carmelites
their rule. The Carmelites' path to divinity was simply to live in allegiance to Jesus Christ, in poverty, in prayer, and in meditation.
By 1400, nuns were allowed to join the order, but some found that it
had strayed from a close, simple allegiance to God. A century and
half later, Teresa de Cepeda y Ahumada, a Castilian, later Saint
Terese of Jesus, a woman who fought illness all her life, who re-

jected then opened herself to divine grace, began a reform of the order. The reform led to a new branch, the Discalced Carmelites, with Saint Terese as the blessed mother.

The nuns on Sixty-sixth Avenue have little contact with the outside world, though they receive messages by voice mail. They pray and meditate regularly. They ring the tower bells at prayer time. They live by Saint Terese and her works, her soul, her courage to create a new order, her final days in the dust-riddled countryside near Salamanca. These sisters remain in communion with God in their simple Italian church overlooking the Pizza Hut at Old York Road, Broad Street, and Sixty-sixth Avenue. The restaurant is standard, senseless architectural fare. Its Italian "red tile roof" is fire engine red and made of rubber. When George brings the sisters their groceries, he leaves the packages on the steps of the church. He rings the bell. I wonder if he notices the smell of pizza as it drifts across the intersection, up and over the old stone walls, and inside the church.

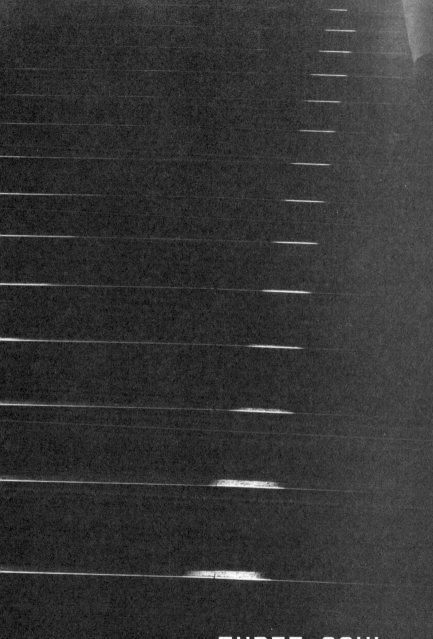

THREE: SOUL

10. THE ENCOUNTER

WE like to assign personality traits to our cities. New York, then, is brash. San Francisco is cool. New Orleans is decadent. San Diego is laid back. Chicago is tough.

Never mind that every city is really millions of stories, layers of human lives. Never mind that no city can be reduced to a single narrative. We believe the labels. We see a city's personality in its buildings. We read it in the faces of its people. We draw it from stories of its sports teams, from the behavior of its politicians, from the quality of its restaurants. As the Philadelphia 76ers climbed to the 2001 National Basketball Association finals, the national media drew parallels between the team and its city. Most of the players in the Sixers starting lineup were injured—some to the degree that they couldn't play. But the broken down team persisted, Rocky-style underdogs fighting for survival, like the city itself.

Like people, cities share basic personality traits. To some degree every city is brash or cool, decadent, laid back, or tough. The traits are relative. They appear in all kinds of combinations. Philadelphia is laid back compared to New York, frenetic and self-important compared to San Diego. But we ignore the combinations, secure in our predetermined labels. No one considers Paris to be a city of fighters. It is too effete, too pretty, too manicured. But in six months living there I sensed as much anger, saw as many fights, heard as many threats as I do in any given year in Philadelphia. Paris is a city of toughs, of outrage, and defended borders.

The personality traits are a result mostly of human density and the diversity of our own personalities, backgrounds, and experiences. The traits are a result of the physical condition of the city too, its body, its location, and its climate. The traits are a function of time. London, now one of the sharpest, hippest cities in the world, was overcrowded and ravaged by the bubonic plague and fire just a little over three centuries ago. Danger lurked in unsanitary water, and in wooden buildings, in so many angry people recently forced off of the commons.

But what about the city's soul? Certainly there is something about the city that evokes from us an emotional, irrational response. There is something powerful in all that glass, brick, and steel and in the life that pulses around us that makes us feel more human, more alive. The city's soul connects us to each other and to generations past, but beyond this it is difficult to understand and describe. It is something we can capture only in the moment of personal interaction, in the face to face of man and city. In that encounter, we find glimpses of the city's soul. Like a human's soul, the city's is not tangible. It is multidimensional and complex; it is personal, revealed to each of us differently. With a gun at his heart, Paul Tucker acted. His action was, in that single moment of a November day, an opening to the city's soul. A boy in the ghetto knows how to respond to danger. He understood then that if he stood frozen on the streets of the Bottom, he would die. In a single moment of self-preservation, Paul revealed something about the soul of Philadelphia. The soul of the city is in the lesson, in the survival instincts, and the quick reflexes. The lessons are taught on a need-to-know basis. They're never entirely revealed. Only the god of places knows the entire soul of Philadelphia. We search for clues. We speculate—and listen, waiting for the city to reveal its secrets, its essence, its soul.

II. AWE

IN our imaginations, fostered in no small part by the sensational media, fear is the most predominant emotion associated with cities. Though automobiles are far more dangerous than cities—and the chance of being killed much higher in the parking lot of a suburban strip mall than on an average corner in any American city—images of the demonic city prevail. Guns, alleys, shadows, and poverty frighten us. We fear situations and people we don't know; we fear random violence.

And we know from Paul Tucker's experience that the city can be a terrifying place. It can send us in a tailspin, heart racing, eyes down, waiting for the crash of glass. It can place us squarely in the hands of trouble. How do we react to the city's terror? Do we grab the gun? Do we shit in our pants? Do we run?

*

At Tulpehocken Station, with my back toward Germantown, the forest rises. It's black against a periwinkle sky. The air smells moist and thick. It's early spring but warm, with a surprising new heat. Even in the car with the windows open, even after discovering that the car's heat had been on still from the morning's chill, even after turning the heat off, the perfect spring air seems uncomfortably warm. Clear in the distance a woodpecker imitates a jackhammer, the jackhammer demolishing the Mayfair Apartments where Frank Sinatra often played and residents of Blue Bell Hill once worked.

The old railroad station is surrounded by apartment buildings that are three, four, five, up to thirteen stories tall. Made from brown and pink brick, the tallest of the apartments was built in the seventies. From a third story window, a man leans out, presses one nostril shut, and shoots snot out the other. A large sign over the circular drive says Four Freedoms House.

In the fields below the station everything blooms yellow—forsythia, daffodil, dandelion, marsh marigold. Thick ivy covers the rough gray bark of the maple trees. Saplings on the edge of the forest have already bloomed, and deep inside, the woods are thick with silver green bud and red twigs. An olive-colored creek sneaks alongside Lincoln Drive. Despite outward signs of spring, the ground is still gray-brown, the last vestige of winter.

When David Young lay bloodied on the cracked and uneven pavement of Tulpehocken Station it was not spring but fall, the time of consequences. He lay there prepared to die with the nineteenth-century station house just behind him. Paint peeling, bricks damaged by age, roof shingles deteriorated, the station was all bright as fluorescent day at nine in the evening. *Fuck you bitch*, someone had written on a Bell Atlantic ad across the tracks.

Between 6:06 A.M. and 11:56 P.M., the Southeastern Pennsylvania Transportation Authority rolls thirty-six trains each way between Germantown and Center City. The fifteen-minute ride follows the original Pennsylvania Railroad route, the line that ran Philadelphians to their summer cottages in the half century after the Civil War. David Young's train arrived at 9:04 P.M. He stepped off the car, and before it pulled away, three men surrounded him. *If you look at anyone we will kill you.* Brandishing guns, they took his wallet and the four dollars inside. Then they beat him. Under the silent forest, the dark-haired historian endured the blows and then waited until the bountyless muggers were gone. He was two blocks from his rented house on Naomi Street in Blue Bell Hill, and his mind swam like the multicolored painted dinosaur doing backstroke on the bridge outside the station.

*

The room in the basement of the old Mission Church is crowded. The air is warm for early November and the dark oak chairs are tightly packed together. Thick, uneven layers of paint cover the walls—the most recent, an ugly mint green. I notice the stained drop ceiling. I watch the South Asian pastor whose eyeglasses are large and unfashionable. She speaks slowly and with a lilt. She shares her dreams for the church and gives out her phone number.

The church is Methodist. Those in attendance are not. Instead, the stuffy basement is filled with past and current residents of Blue Bell Hill. They have covered a table at the back of the room with curled brown and white photographs. At the front, the oldest are discussing out-of-use street names, the pretty little names of the Rittenhouse girls, and the woods, always the woods. *We ran through the woods, we knew every inch. We would hang our clothes on the tree branches and swim in the creek so clear you could see every stone and every naked body.*

It is David Young's night. He presides over the third neighborhood history night, the fruit of four years' enchantment with his adopted home. At first it must have been the genuineness of the people, Saturdays on the park bench with Clem Rittenhouse, listening to his two-hundred-year old stories. Maybe it was Gene Aucott, fit like a bull with his motorcycles and his walks to the spring—the last existing fresh drinking water supply in the city. The stories told to David, a suburban boy who longed for meaning in his surroundings, enveloped him. David found a place for himself in Blue Bell Hill. An enormous forest wraps around Blue Bell Hill on three sides. David has learned these woods, in terms of both natural and human history. He found the first stagecoach pass to Roxborough. He climbed to the sites of the taverns and the mills. He located the caves and old creek beds.

In the church, David stands before his neighbors. Nearly two months have passed since the assault at the station. Before that there was another mugging, that time by teenagers. Prior to that, the first incident took place on a spring day while David and his wife, Sloane, and their son, Stanton, were at a cabin in French Creek State Park. Men pulled up to his house with a van, crow-barred open the door, and walked out with all their belongings. A neighbor drove out to the park to tell them. Everyone on the block helped with replacements. But still he wondered, how could no one have seen this happen, or stopped it or called the police?

On this night set aside to honor the neighborhood, David Young, whose dark brown hair is combed to the side, is as joyful as a child, as much in love as the happiest groom on his wedding day. He has endured the city's terror. The burglary was a jab to the ribs. It shook him. The first mugging was like a soft punch to the face. It caught his attention like an annoying fly. The armed assault at Tupel-hocken Station knocked him down. But here he stands.

David's scabs have healed and he no longer aches. But he re-members lying on the pavement on the bottom of the hill from his house prepared to die, prepared to hear a crack and then nothing else again. Tonight he is the neighborhood's greatest champion and he swoons with love.

David's story provides a view into the city's soul. Lying on the sidewalk by the train tracks, David was terrorized but also alive. The city brought him to the brink and then let him go. Is this the power of God? He bled onto the pavement, but the force of his own attachment to the city, to Blue Bell Hill, and to his neighbors kept him going. David's blood was the spirit of his resolve, an out-pouring of love for the city. He had really sacrificed something now. His blood shared the same earth with mill hands and log-gers, with pioneers. The city took from him but sustained him with its history. This is the soul of the city at its purest. It de-

mands we give our lives as it nourishes us. The city threatens us as
it fills us with delight.

David begins to speak to his neighbors about his relationship
with Blue Bell Hill. The fabric of the place has forcibly seized him.
Blue Bell Hill has always had a separatist flavor. Less affluent than
the rest of Germantown, the neighborhood is physically cut off by
the forest, the creek, and by Lincoln Drive. It is a marginal place
tucked into the forest, a dense city neighborhood the police have
difficulty finding. For years until the Walnut Lane Bridge was built,
the only way to Germantown was over a rickety span that crossed
Lincoln Drive. Hucksters used to fill the streets of Blue Bell Hill,
bringing goods and services, a trail of sheep, and the noise and
smell of traveling peddlers.

David's wife Sloane stumbled on the inexpensive house on
Naomi in 1995. A year later, he was immersed in the history of his
new neighborhood. Slowly, neighbor-to-neighbor, he uncovered its
story. David interviewed every neighbor who would take the time,
researched the schools and churches, the neighborhood institutions, and the architecture. He crafted an oral history of Blue Bell
Hill, the project that made his career, probably earned him the job
as the education director of the city's history museum. He tells that
history with a storyteller's eye, and the thrill of human wonder.
*Imagine the smell and the dust! Livestock all around, and the streets
were not paved then. The sidewalks were wooden. And geography matters! Imagine how difficult it was just to get to Germantown.*

He feels the measure of this community on Sunday afternoons
walking along Naomi or Kingsley or Daniel, not missing a play of
the Eagles game. The announcer's voice heard from every house.
He feels the force of the neighborhood's history as he walks along
these streets. He senses that history as it mingles with the present.
Old stories of Blue Bell Hill wind like a clinging vine around the
houses and trees. Naomi Street is the oldest in Blue Bell Hill, and

the original houses were built into the hillside early in the nineteenth century. At one end where rusted stairs lead down to Daniel Street and the old dairy barn, where a red wooden fence covered in grape vines matches the hemlocks and autumnal red maples, stands a wine-colored fifties brick apartment building. Across from the Russian scientist's stone and stucco house, where a couch sits on the front porch, are four grim eighties townhouses thankfully built at the same small scale of the street and set close to the sidewalk. The houses are covered in melba brown vinyl siding, with chocolate on the trim. A grape-colored Chrysler Neon is parked outside. Naomi is tight like a hallway. It is an organic swath of single and twin houses in bright white stucco, with Germantown schist retaining walls lined with impatiens, pumpkins, blue plastic pails of faded begonias, and scampering black and white cats. Along the shared stoops where hosta grows and faded American flags dangle, only the muffled sound of a vacuum cleaner might break the silence.

On any given day, neighbors float back and forth across the street, in and out of kitchens, drinking coffee and beer. The evening someone spotted a dead body in a car, everyone came out to see. Dick Reeves takes care of things around the neighborhood. He painted Kim Miller's house. He mows her lawn in back and prunes the trees along the street. The youngest on the street when they moved into Dick's grandparent's house in 1949, Frankie and Dick Reeves have probably lived on Naomi the longest. The house was the last to get indoor plumbing, in 1947. Theirs was the second car on the street. At the cluttered white Formica kitchen table, Dick drains cans of Coors Light while listening to local right-populist talk radio host Michael Smerconish. Frankie, a Californian, stands by the sink. She thinks former mayor (and once frequent guest on the radio show) Frank Rizzo was brilliant. *I don't care what anyone says.* Their son died of an overdose the day before Rizzo was taken by a heart attack in a restroom while running for a third term. Their daughter Patty owns the house next door.

This is David Young's neighborhood. He knows everyone's story. On a piece of paper he could chart the layers of human lives here. He knows where everyone stands. He knows how a Rittenhouse once married a Catholic. He has heard Frankie Reeves say, *we have always had black families living here and they never knew prejudice until they left.* He has sat with Bunny, a black old-timer, who said she has never been as comfortable as when she lived in Blue Bell Hill. He knows about the hot breath of police horses on the necks of necking teenagers. He knows how one of the teenagers became a nun.

Now he knows the woods. He spends weekends there with his son Stanton, exploring, sledding by the Thomas mansion, gathering the scene like a collector of human moments. The Wissahickon Gorge is relentless beauty, steep slate colored rock, beech, maple, ash, elm, and oak. Rocky cliffs overlook small sandy beaches. Horseback riders, bikers, runners, walkers, and hikers all claim their space along Forbidden Drive. On a walk with David through his woods we smell a sewage wind blowing off the creek. We slide on wet brown leaves. Under foot a bamboo rod cracks. We step over a Cheetos bag, rusted Colt 45 can, black winter coat, and one lonely peach-colored penis-shaped squash growing in a grove. We smell autumn and the black earth. We spot an extensive stash of beer bottles neatly arranged and lined up under the bridge.

The neighborhood contains this human ecology. Naomi Street is as cute as a television show's set—simple picket-fence American vernacular. But it is worn. It endures chainsaws and chickens and bad paint jobs. The street passively records every moment. On an autumn night, forty-eight hours after David was beaten at the station, I observe Naomi Street—nothing exceptional happens, just life as it befalls the street. More than anything, the moment presents us with a picture of people living in a place, together. To David, this is what matters. Not the extraordinary beauty of the forest itself, but the point where we as human beings insert ourselves into it. It is no consecrated act, but hard, dirty, and dangerous. Men once lived in caves here, if only to survive a little longer. Was it worth the flight from their homeland? Are the hours sledding with Stanton worth his own blood on the ground? David answers yes. Blue Bell Hill buzzes with a human value worth perhaps every last possession, the mugging, and a swift preparation to die on a muggy evening under the florescent buzz.

Belonging to a place is not just a function of personal history. David Young moved to Germantown because his wife found an affordable house to rent there. Good soil supports non-native species. The best transplants respect those growing there already. So David has thrived in Blue Bell Hill, his own sense of belonging comes from his appreciation for the special human ecology of the neighborhood, for the people and houses, streets and hills, for the streams and woods that surround him. This awe is his window to the city, the basis for a personal, unrestrained connection to a place. It is, also, one way we can view the city's soul.

*

As David sits at home recovering from the beating, midway down the block, Kim Miller, who once found herself sharing an Australian villa with Bill Gates' girlfriend, helps her neighbor Nadia with her homework. They are upstairs in Nadia's comfortable living room. Pillows are arranged neatly on the couch. Nadia sits at the desk writing answers to a worksheet of questions, a reading comprehension exercise. She'd rather be rolling on the worn carpet with Amir the Australian shepherd, a big baby of a dog who doesn't stop and crouch to shit but keeps right on walking. Nadia's parents have just left for after-school night. They left with an evening course schedule on a yellow sheet: French/Spanish, language arts, social studies, math, and science. Nadia's mother, Mary, grew up in this two-hundred-year-old house on Naomi. Her parents bought it for ten thousand dollars in 1952. When her mother died in 1984, she felt no other pull but to move back to Naomi. Where else would she go?

Nadia's father Ibrahim was raised in the eastern Atlas Mountains, in a village named for the Moors who came east to escape the terror of Queen Isabella in Spain. Ibrahim himself escaped the brutal dictatorship in Tripoli and met Mary at a campus bar in West Philadelphia. After visas back and forth and hot, absorbing summers together in Morocco, he now spends an intellectual's life, reading and taking notes in tiny, dense script.

Nadia finishes the reading lesson. They take Amir out to the street for a walk. She and Kim cross Naomi, pass the Reeves's and Mary Ellen and Gary's double house. Kim knocks on Kara's door. *I thought you were going to join us for book club*, and Kim, *I know but I just forgot.* Amir pulls Nadia into the house and Kim and Kara talk on the stoop. Kim leaves with a lamp Kara no longer wants and asks, *What about the Bruce show on Thursday night?* Out to the street with the stainless lamp, the dog pulls the eleven-year-old to a chorus of yelping and giggling. A car pulls up. It's Kara's friend Tamara who cannot come in for book night either. This is a moment in the dark quiet fall air: the dog, the girl, an oversized lamp, a car, and voices now, always, a part of the street.

*

Kathy Paulmier was raised on Baynton Street, back behind Germantown Avenue, wedged up against the train line to Trenton. Baynton is leafy and giving. The large silver-stone, Germantown schist, Victorian houses exhibit flourishes, turrets, and plenty of shady porches. The houses on Baynton sit high above the street.

The small trees of Kathy's youth are now enormous. They drape the houses. The effect is dripping wet and green, overgrown, almost shabby like a Truman Capote house in a steamy southern summer. Lilac and dogwood grow close to the street. Mostly black professionals lived on Baynton Street in the sixties along with Kathy's family and a few other whites too progressive, tolerant, or lazy to move. Perhaps they never saw that predicted drop in real estate values or perhaps Quaker *values* held forth. After all it was only a few blocks away at Germantown and Wister where on February 18, 1688—177 years before the Emancipation Proclamation—Quakers who had been driven from Calvinist Europe signed a protest against slavery in Pennsylvania:

> *There is a saying that we shall to all men like as we will be done ourselves; making no difference of what generation, descent of or colour they are. And those who steal or robb men, and those who buy or purchase them, are they not alike? Here is liberty of conscience which is right and reasonable; here ought to be likewise liberty of ye body. . . . But to bring men hither, or to robb or sell them against their will, we stand against. In Europe there are many oppressed for conscience sake; and here there are those oppressed who are of black color. . . . Pray, what thing in the world can be done worse towards us, than if men should robb or steal us away, and sell us for slavers in strange countries; separating husbands from their wives and children. Being now this is not done in the manner we would be done at therefore we contradict and are against this traffik of men-body.*

Kathy Paulmier keeps faded copies of the 1688 Germantown Protest in her small office. The deep brown wood doors seem out of place in a Quaker institution, which is more often typified by plain, unadorned walls and simplicity. Whole sections of the one-page protest have been underlined, important paragraphs highlighted;

the sheet has been mimeographed a thousand times. At the top someone has written, *Ask three or four students to read aloud.*

Kathy's face is square, her hair dirty blond, her eyes hazel, her voice soft but determined. She is the director of community involvement at Germantown Friends, the prekindergarten to twelfth grade school from which she and her husband graduated. Germantown Friends was her grandmother's and her parents' school and has always been the place where her family has attended Sunday meeting. Her own children go to school there now.

The protest is like a talisman at Germantown Friends. For a school that strives to be open and progressive, the protest is 314-year-old proof of its values. It is a statement read over and over, rehashed and explained, debated and dissected. It is the ability to stand on the spot, three blocks away, where the school's very ancestors claimed moral ground. The protest is ephemeral and real. It serves as the jumping point for schoolwide discussions of race. It gives Kathy credibility in a mostly black neighborhood. Race relations are her personal struggle, the uncertain dimension she has been called to explore.

*

The snow had started sometime early in the morning and by daybreak the ground was covered. Wind blows the snow across the landscape. Mist covers the Schuylkill River, whose waters swirl and splash. A photographer who has waited for this feverish moment has brought out his large format camera. Here he stands in the gray embrace at Kelly Drive and Sedgwick Avenue in the shadow of Abraham Lincoln, the black of the camera a magicians box in this April trick. Just a day before the thermometer had registered seventy-five.

Snow is plastered to old Abe, a favorite of this Union city, as he watches over the art museum and the delicate, handsome boathouses along the river. Snow covers General Grant's hat, Mayor Rizzo's broad shoulders, and Jack Kelly's oars. Green leaves have been transformed into winter silhouettes with black bark and white branches stretching over the street. The cars lining the streets of East Falls and Germantown are tightly parked and snow covered, strung along, it seems, like a 1940s photograph of a neighborhood street.

Kathy and Chris Paulmier and Carter, who is seven, and Melia, aged five, live on Baynton Street, two doors down from Kathy's parents. I trudge through muddy landscaping, past outbuildings, a snow-covered picnic table, and woody shrubs bending under the weight of the morning's upheaval to find them there. The wide porch of their converted carriage house is level to the ground. It blends into the woody scenery. The porch is crowded with bikes, an old stove, building materials, toys, and an air-propelled rocket that won't fly far.

Carter is a dusty blond, straight-faced boy. In the morning's snow he wears tall boots. If he were two feet taller, he would hold an axe in his hand, cutting firewood for the Olympic Crest stove in the living room. Instead, he brings his mother snow-covered red and yellow tulips from the yard. She places them in a glass. Carter and Melia's artwork hangs all around the messy, rich-coffee scented, Sunday morning kitchen; there are easels, and a computer rests on the wide windowsill near the counter. Tall pussy willow cuttings stand in a vase. A wet piney smell from the stove fills the house.

Chris Paulmier is still bed-headed, his face covered by a couple of days' growth. He rebuilt the kitchen, transformed it from a dark and useless place. The old stove has a push-button pilot and porcelain knobs, like those on a sink, to open the gas. After meeting, three families new to the meetinghouse will be coming for lunch. It was supposed to have been a picnic.

Visible from the living room, where a portrait of Rosa Parks hangs near a caged zebra finch and an old worn flowery couch, is a one-acre stand of trees and nettle, the Palumier's small forest of towering tulip and gingko trees, one of which counts as the second oldest in the state. A sign in red ink taped to the inside of the front door reads:

SIX (6) STEPS TO SCHOOL
get dressed
eat breakfast
do jobs
put on shoes
put on coat
take lunch and backpack

The four Paulmiers, still in Sunday morning casual clothes, push out through the door, off to meeting. The walk to meeting grounds Kathy. It helps her shed the material world. And more, it is the same Sunday walk she took as a girl with her parents. This walk is a chance to see her neighborhood, quiet on a Sunday, seemingly unchanged from her childhood. This ordinary stroll is her moment to see the community of Friends coming together, converging for one special hour. It is ritual opportunity to greet neighbors and reconnect with her past. Today she is sparked by vivid memories of picking up her grandmother at Penn and Knox Streets in snow storms and helping her get to meeting. Meeting never closes, even in the heaviest of snow. Together, the walk and then meeting is Kathy's source of strength and will, a weekly renewing.

The walk is short and simple: down Baynton to Coulter, past Lena Street and then to Germantown Avenue where towering oaks surround the meetinghouse. On this Sunday with the wind blowing snow and shaking newly blooming trees, the familiar streets appear different. The air smells like winter; the scene is disorienting. Near Kathy's parents' house snow drapes the fir trees and ices the budding lilacs. The sidewalk is a gray slushy mess. Wet pelting snow seems to come from all sides. The tops of the trees in a churchyard sweep wildly like palms in a hurricane. A car alarm sounds. Squinting our eyes, discussing theology, we put our heads down and walk on.

Quakers live by five principals: peace, simplicity, community, quality, and integrity. *It's hard to be a Quaker!* Kathy sighs. *Nearly impossible. It's impossible not to be a Quaker*, retorts her husband.

In 1652, George Fox, an Englishman, had a vision of a direct knowledge of God, a knowledge not merely reserved for clergy, but for anyone willing to open up to God's continual presence, to forget the canon and instead seek constantly unfurling revelation. The first meetings came to be early acts of democracy in a brutal nation rapidly enslaving its people. Each Quaker ministered the word of God, reliant on his personal relationship with God, the teachings in the Bible, and the communal standards set out by the meeting. To the earliest Quakers, the word of God was always changing, being challenged and questioned, and out of the silence of the meetinghouse it was spoken.

Coulter Street is filled with two-story row houses graced by porches and three-story Victorians with carved wood on the eaves and terrazzo flowers. Avon products crowd a window. *Danger Keep Out* is printed on a burnt orange sign screwed to the plywood window on a deserted house. A chain-link fence stretches back through the alley. At Lena, the corner store is almost in ruins.

Outside the meetinghouse a New England January seems to hover. With the smell of wood smoke, everything is given back to winter, at least for a few hours. We find the fire inside and an old building smell, and the Friends all clad in sweaters and boots. The meetinghouse is comprised of four earth-colored walls with a ceiling for cover. The pews are aligned in a square with tall windows on one side. We can enter the stubborn silence of the meeting from either side. The trees outside the window can be heard brushing the sudsy sky. We hear a siren pass, legs shuffling.

The Friends sit in personal contemplation, in William Penn's nourishing silence, hands up, open to God. The silence continues. Eyes are closed or open, blank or lively. No one giggles, makes a face, doubts the endeavor, and Kathy stands. Some respond and gaze up, others just listen. Chris faces straight ahead, no smile of recognition. Melia sits next to Kathy on the bench. She squirms hearing her mother in peaceful resolution, seeking and open. Melia climbs into the back of Kathy's sweater, while Chris's blue eyes remain far away, in a trance.

Kathy holds out her hands, open, facing up, and she speaks chokingly of E.B. White. Paraphrasing the essayist, she says, *When I get up in the morning I don't know whether to enjoy the world or to save it*. She too, she says slowly, faces this same dilemma. She feels alone and helpless. But meeting each week always helps her. She is comforted by the communal search for truth. Her voice quivers, but no one cries out. She sits down.

The children stay for fifteen minutes, after which they leave for school. Their shuffling shatters the silence, but not the peace. Carter leads Melia out of the square of worship. A few minutes later a man who sits on the right of the room notes the comfort he feels as he hears Kathy speak, a voice he has known since first grade. I am reminded that this old meetinghouse is really a delirious web of personal connections. They come here each Sunday as much to listen to each other minister the word of God as to hear each other's voices. They come to look into hazel eyes, to stare at wrinkles, to grasp dry hands, all of them familiar, all of them a reflection of themselves and the city where they live. Sitting on hard wooden benches, of course they look inside, they search, they ponder. They look inside themselves and see among other things the soul of their city. They see the remarkable, insatiable city that contains every instant, every breath, and every dimension of their lives.

When Kathy stood in the silent meetinghouse, she posed an existential question, really also a moral one. Is it better to enjoy the world or serve it? Is it better to run and help others or stay and listen?

Home alone on Baynton Street at eighteen, Kathy answered a knock. Moments later she was shot and raped by a drug-fueled man. That is when she ran. She ran to California to attend Stanford. She ran with Chris to Japan to teach and do mission work. She ran as far from home as possible, staying away for thirteen years.

And then Kathy returned to Germantown. By deciding to return, she was recognizing something about the city's soul, its unquenchable appetite for lives. Only the city had the power to hold her. She might have been living in Japan, but the streets of Germantown possessed her past, her family, and her relationships with God and people. She could not stay away. She would circle her life around the meeting, her anchor, and she let the meeting guide her. She understood at once the meaning and the messages. It was a homecoming, time to face the dirty breath of life.

*

Kathy sits in the courtyard at Germantown Friends with stands of oak, maple, and elm all around. She is dressed as if for prep school—rolled-up tweed sleeves with leather patches on the elbows. The sun is warm on the picnic table, and it's lunchtime. The remains of someone's birthday cake have been left to the bees. An ad hoc soccer game roars around the picnic tables. The courtyard bustles with adolescent energy. Stillness settles only as classes resume. Kathy sits in the courtyard of the school where her grandmother was graduated in 1908, and here her life rests in one place: meeting, family, work, and school.

To understand something about the soul of the city we must consider not just the power of the city to hold our lives, but what it means to live each day as part of a landscape. Kathy herself is like the meetinghouse. She is like the gingko trees that grow behind her house. She is like the Victorian houses that line the brick sidewalks. She is like those sidewalks too, part of the bedrock of Germantown. Kathy belongs to Germantown. Belonging is the one human emotion that can quell doubt. It can erase terror, ease a constant grasping, and smooth disquieting ambition. When Kathy realized where she belonged, she stopped running. She reached into the ground that is northwest Philadelphia and found her family, her own past, and her values.

Recognizing and abiding by Kathy's sense of belonging to Germantown has simplified her life. Yet no one's relationship with the city is simple. The city is far too dynamic and ever changing. It is an elusive lover. Kathy poses existential questions in the meetinghouse, seeking guidance. The Germantown she returned to is not the place she fled. Her part of the neighborhood, though in her lifetime always integrated, is now almost entirely inhabited by African Americans. It is poor. They discuss racial relations frequently at the dinner table. Carter and Melia wonder why their neighborhood friends are mostly black, but schoolmates are predominantly white. When Kathy took Melia to swimming lessons at the Y on Germantown Avenue, where she learned to swim herself, she found that the place had closed two weeks before for lack of funding. The great old department stores are defunct, replaced by lesser quality discount outfits. Still she belongs here, covering and recovering the tracks of her childhood, enraptured even as she doubts and struggles. On any day in Germantown, we might catch Kathy Paulmier on her bicycle, riding up and down Germantown Avenue. She is shopping and eating, entering the meetinghouse, walking the halls of Germantown Friends. She is living here, seeking her own peace, asking for guidance, and listening. She knows the answers are here. For her, there is no place else they can be.

12. THE STUCCO WALL

AS a newspaperman Steve Honeyman learned about power and money. Working for a paper in Missouri he wrote an award-winning piece on a local nuclear power plant, a story about gross mismanagement and danger. The article brought immediate attention to the problem and praise for the writer, from everyone, it seemed, but the publisher of the newspaper. The publisher, as it turned out, was an investor in the menacing nuclear plant.

Many years later, Steve began to work in Philadelphia, in the old districts along the Delaware. Now he organizes neighbors in Fishtown, in the Barrio, in Olney and Richmond. He brings people together, people with extraordinary ideas about how they, as residents, can change the city. He develops systems and organizing structures, boards, committees, and he trains hundreds of residents to be leaders, charting the course of each neighborhood's future. The neighbors write plans and account for the future of their schools. He helps them elucidate shared values, while engaging neighborhood institutions like churches, hospitals, and schools.

Steve Honeyman's beard and long ponytail are gray. He sits in the organizing office, an old classroom, on the third floor of the school at the Visitation Blessed Virgin Mary Church. He smokes one cigarette after the next. The bilingual administrator answers the phone that seems to never stop ringing. With organizational diagrams drawn on the chalkboard, plans for the future of places settled centuries ago sit before him. His organizers are inheritors of the city, the city that once grew in terrible ambition, that once consumed everything around it, and generated its own power and wealth. But Steve Honeyman's organizers are not, like those first

153

Europeans to settle here, cogs in a new capital-creating machine. Actually, they are more at liberty to create communities that reflect their own personal, and also shared, sense of the world.

The residents are brilliant dreamers. They envision a transparent, wonderful city. They envision trees and playgrounds, safe streets, and great schools. They envision democracy and mutual respect. They envision a city that supports cultural traditions and strong neighborhood voices. Steve only wishes to give them the tools. The student of power structures and institutions, he is the stark and bitten realist. He clearly sees the tension that holds still this constant negotiation. He arms the residents with tools, and together they dream and fight the power.

Steve organizes people to place value in themselves and their neighborhoods, to understand and respect the history of the place where they live, to believe that they deserve justice and fair attention from city hall. He teaches them that their power is only as forceful as they are compelling. He teaches them to negotiate, to take no one as a permanent ally and no one as a permanent enemy. He advises them that they will lose many battles and that the war itself might never end. To make this point, the organizer calls on his own experience and the wisdom of the father of neighborhood organizing, Saul Alinsky. To understand power and ultimately to take it, *always follow the dollar.*

*

Daryl Gale is *City Paper*'s first African American reporter, the Rosa Parks of the newsroom, as he jokes. Years before he was Air Force Radio's voice of Guantánamo Bay, Cuba. He is a big, good-natured, confident, and perceptive man who feeds on the everyday stories he sees around him. He laughs deeply but not easily, having seen too much for idle giggles. He worked his way onto the *City Paper* staff by challenging editor Howard Altman to diversify the news crew after hearing Howard questioned on the subject by Mary Mason, a black talk radio host who likes to kick up dust. The editor responded and the two men started to correspond. Then came invitations to submit articles and finally a staff position.

Daryl likes to play a little game at night on the street. If he passes a white woman walking alone, he turns away, pretends to be frightened. Some women get the joke, they laugh or smile. With them, he has a silent conversation about race and fear, about expectations of the behavior of black men, and as usual he asks the women to look at things a little differently, this time to turn them upside down. *Everyone is trained to believe that everything that happens in Philadelphia happens in Center City*, he says, leaning forward, coffee in hand—a hand that smells of cigarettes. But in this town it is the neighborhoods that hold his interest, not downtown, and those neighborhoods are difficult to clearly define. *Good and bad don't mean anything. We have poor whites in Kensington and rich blacks in Overbrook Farms. It doesn't break down along traditional lines.*

Daryl is out to report on his Philadelphia, to write the diary of the neighborhoods, to spread the paper's reach to the corners of the north, south, and west sections of the city, where the diversity of people and stories seem limitless. In fields and streets of row houses and apartment buildings, along elevated tracks, where the trolley ambles, in corner bars like Susie's Rusty Nail and Johnny Moo's, the writer finds the endless city. He collects mounds of material and countless lead characters like needles on a porcupine's back ready to prick our robot senses and perhaps draw a little blood.

In Daryl's city we find Larry Falcon, the Forty-third Street minister whose soul belongs in open country fields, whose heart is welded to the people around him, who preaches a comfort zone to the kids on the street, and who has seen firsthand the death scourge of crack and life anxiety. Here too is Abdoviaziz Ahmed, owner of Abby's Desert Lounge on Baltimore Avenue, Daryl's favorite neighborhood taproom. Here in Daryl Gale's city is Pork Chops, a steady working family man, a *dogman*, a muscular forty-two-year-old who raises pit bulls for deadly fights and cash. Pork Chops' dog Rufus is his pride. Undefeated so far in three snatches, the dog is still alive or has not been badly maimed in a fight. The fights are often in someone's dark basement or garage. But Rufus is young, still in training to learn to grip harder on the neck of another pit, and still she has a way to prove Pork Chops' muster, his bravado.

For the pit bull story, editor Howard Altman put Daryl on the cover for the second time, with a picture of the white-pink mouth of the pit, wet tongue, studded collar, and eyes bent on the kill. Dogman, digger, cur, nuts, heavy mouth, a snatch: this is the lingo in the world of pit bulls by Daryl Gale. Daryl's story on pit bulls was well wrung and balanced. On a subject that any writer could have butchered into a singular diatribe against the killer animals and the brutal indecency of the dogmen, Gale captured all sides of the ritual. He meted out the S.P.C.A. response, how city politics keeps the issue out of the public agenda, how dangerous the dogs are to public health. But the dogmen are men after all, some like Pork Chops are smart and sincere but too far gone to see the sport for the brutality that it represents. Others are too dumb to obey basic rules and common sense. Some are new to the craft, learning how to care for and love the dogs, while turning them into tortured fighting machines.

When editor Altman handed his newest reporter a letter written by a woman named Tremain Smith, he knew he had a real David versus Goliath story. Altman thought the story would resonate across the city. The letter stated that a group of neighbors in West Philadelphia was organizing to fight the building of a McDonald's they felt would destroy the fabric of their community. What's more, the zoning board approved the project despite the fact that neighbors collected over two hundred petition signatures against it. Local politicians were silent; neighbors, tenants, and workers in the factory the McDonald's would replace were kept in the dark until one day the deal was done.

What concerned the neighbors was not only that the city had ignored their attempts to control the course of their own neighborhood, but also the specific results of the new development itself. The McDonald's was to be wedged into the traditional urban pattern that defined their neighborhood. They saw what was coming: grimy asphalt, desiccated concrete parking spot barriers, yellow lines, the floating flotsam of corporate junk greeting the sidewalk pedestrian, and the low-slung, pathetic building pushed back on the lot. And they knew that poor neighborhoods like theirs were the most susceptible to this unkind demonstration of urban investment. How the politicians love the fresh paint, spacious aisles, colorful spray-on stucco, sterile mulch, *juniperus horizontalis, thuja orientalis,* neon signs, and all.

A two-story window factory on the south side of Market Street is the designated site. The Elevated heaves above here on seventy-year-old rickety steel tracks. Along the street is Stan's Fix-a-Flat, M and T Furniture, Pep Boys, Midas Mufflers, the old television studio where Dick Clark became America's oldest living teenager and where Paul Tucker now publishes a fashion magazine. A block from the Mickey D's-to-be is a red, yellow, and green K.F.C. Outside, an animated and courtly plantation boss offers dollar-ninety-nine sandwiches, tender roast and extra crunchy. The side wall of a row house facing the K.F.C. parking lot, behind green and white plastic flags, is covered by a mural of a small farm, probably a community garden. There are rows of peppers, lettuce, orange ripening tomatoes, a woman and a small child in the fields. At the front of the scene is an older black couple, arms around each other, faces chiseled into a stare of pride. She is holding a field mix of daisies and asters. And there is a harvest basket filled with corn, pumpkins, peppers, onion, garlic, eggplant, and cabbage.

The McDonald's is to be set back from the street midblock with parking and a drive-thru entrance in front. The fried, grizzle-reeking plume will drift from behind the handsome row houses on Forty-third Street, the ghetto malt liquor stop-n-go on the corner, and the massive English-style Episcopal cathedral at Chestnut Street. But the vile odor is not the neighbors' chief concern.

Daryl Gale learns this as he boils down the McDonald's story. On a clear, cool Friday morning in April, the journalist returns to Forty-third Street for secondary interviews, to see for himself what the neighbors fear they will lose. Daryl finds clues outside Larry Falcon's house. Falcon is a Cajun reverend, the voice of the neighborhood, the organizer, leader, and moral talisman. He serves a small church and a school that his wife runs, and they operate a thrift shop around the corner. Larry is like a mad angel, a traveling huckster, a medicine man. His long straight hair is white as is his Fu Manchu goatee. His lilt is country Louisiana, his commitment to the community and especially the children is clear. He takes as little as he can from the world. Everything around him has been owned by someone else first. On this day in April, and any other, he—like Kathy Paulmier in Germantown—is a fixture just like the streets and buildings themselves.

On the edge of the sidewalk in front of Larry's house are broken down benches. They face the house. He has built a small garden, planted rose of Sharon, a pale pink cherry tree and built a birdbath. An old southern metal porch chair and a tree stump sit to the left of the stoop. Plastic weatherproofing is stapled to the door. Lines of terra-cotta detail adorn the buildings on this block, which are designed with center hall doorways and dining rooms in front windows.

Daryl sits with Larry under the front window at the sticky wood table. The oven door is open, providing heat to the house. Dried chili peppers hang in the corner and old iron skillets decorate the archway into the kitchen. A bare long-life bulb hangs from the ceiling fan. Morning light filters through the window. Larry talks about ancient cities, biblical cities, places considered protected and safe, gardens inside the fortress walls. He himself runs a community garden called F.A.I.T.H. (Food Always in the House). He mentions the diversity of the neighbors, who are close-knit but not in your face. Larry talks about how crack has plowed through the community. His wife lost her best friend in a shooting. He talks about how they finally beat back crack and shut down the drug house, how he took the local kids to the ocean and the country—and how afraid the children were in the uncomposed woods away from the protection of the street. He describes the annual block party and the venison—the Bambi burgers that no one would eat. Daryl records everything in clean bent-around-the-pen, left-handed script.

Maria Kotsikoros is the *City Paper* photographer assigned to the story. She is young, dressed in black, with Barbie pink nails. She arrives soon after Larry's neighbor, Wren Ingram. A manager of a trendy restaurant, Wren is in her forties. Wren brings a poster board of photographs. The pictures are of the gardens behind the Forty-third Street houses. The pictures show what McDonald's plans to take away.

The garden behind Larry's house is large and shady. Reverend Falcon built an oasis, a family spot for dinner and long, warm evenings. Its brick paths and partially melted candles, ferns, a fountain and pond feel like a New Orleans terrace. A dinner bell, yellow daffodils, an old stone face, and an old-fashioned tool collection make the garden seem gentle and carefree.

This early in spring, Larry's turtle, named Aya-turtle during the Iran hostage crisis, is still hibernating. Really he is hiding for his life. His habitat will be destroyed when the fast food restaurant is built. The stucco, ivy-covered wall that defines the eastern edge of the garden, that also protects it and lends charm and security, is part of the factory that is to be demolished. The messy, ruinous demolition will likely kill Aya-turtle. The property lines will be readjusted, the garden itself will shrink. A chain-link fence with green plastic strips covering the holes will serve as the new back garden wall and beyond it the parking lot and the McDonald's itself. The character of the place, its essence, will be, as Larry says this morning, *McBurglered.*

Wren looks downcast as she poses for Maria's camera in front of the pond she built ten years before. In the paper the following Thursday, she looks lost, swallowed by the gray creeper vines on the wall. Her pond looks like a black hole. Never mind the comet fish and the frog, the nesting birds, grackers, catbirds, sparrows, and cardinals. Never mind the sweet honeysuckle, chocolate mint, anis, woodruff, lavender, Thai basil, purple sage, and French tarragon.

A week after the tour of the doomed sites, Gale's article runs in the *City Paper.* The neighbors' voices are projected, just enough perhaps to raise the issue to citywide concern. And Daryl captures the wretched company's bullshit, the carefully crafted contempt. "From our perspective, that site is part of McDonald's overall commitment to the city of Philadelphia, through which we'll continue to bring jobs and investment to the city." Daryl found the right to be blowhard. "We're investing in the future of that community."

For years the neighbors have worked to make this city their own. They have labored day and night to make streets safer, to rescue their children. The neighbors teach love and understanding. They open their doors. They stand, still, until the drug dealers finally walk away. And they tend gardens. They took the ugly, worn wall of the old factory, where every day men come to earn wages making windows, and turned it into charm and delight. The city has relented to their touch, its hard edges have softened. Though so much of the beauty is hidden from the street, the garden brings peace to the whole block. Only now the city turns away, grabbing easy money—and from the dirtiest John.

The city trades love for grease and low wages. It trades an unwavering commitment for empty words. It lies, throwing the whole affair in our collective face. The bewitching city provokes us. But just as it is about to abandon us, it looks back. We look up and respond. Do we sell our houses and move out? Yes, some do. The rest of us keep dreaming. We organize, plan, and fight. Like Kathy Paulmier, we dig in deeper. The reaction is irrational; we keep loving the city. Damn this beguiling place! Damn it as we take our evenings not for gardening but for organizing and petitioning. Why do we bother? How can we stop? Unwaveringly compelling, the city doesn't let us. We can't say no. So we embrace the city if for nothing else but to mark our time here. We grow our own vines; we decorate our own wall. Beneath them are pitted, worn bricks, some chipped and orange, and bubbles of stucco and vines, the first buds of spring. We imagine the countless seasons that have passed over this factory's side wall. We recognize the magnitude of the city. It provokes us to fight and make our mark, to be remembered. There is no other way.

We know why we fight. The spirit of the city is too great for us. Even as it rejects our love, it entices us. Through the layers of the partially crumbling stucco wall, where brick and mortar are visible, where dirt and paint have collected over generations, the city speaks to us. Like the layers of the wall, the city's soul is vast; it is a whore and an artist, an inventor, a king. It overwhelms us with the force of human history.

Daryl's article galvanizes the neighbors on Forty-third Street. Acting under the name North of Chestnut Organized Neighbors (N.O.C.O.N.), they plan a protest for the following Friday at four in the afternoon. The day turns out to be grand. Warm and relaxed, the neighborhood is in an early spring, early weekend state of contentment. In the strong sun, everyone on the street laughs and jokes. Firefighters across Market Street sit on bright benches. A fire truck, resplendent and shiny, sticks its head out of a garage bay. As four o'clock nears, the stop-n-go picks up. The sign outside the door says, *Old English 2000 Step to the Real*.

Larry and Wren come out first to the corner. They set down their hand-written white poster board signs so that they can set up a small table with information and petitions to sign. The *City Paper* is stacked eight high and open to the article. They display one copy of a scholarly piece that describes the brutal local economics of a McDonald's franchise. Seems that the company is the largest land-holder in the world. Most franchisees pay rent to the big corporation in addition to franchise fees. The author estimates that 80 percent of the store's profits escape the local community, leaving only the smell of charred grease at the end of the day.

Characteristically, Larry flies around the sidewalk, hope burning through his small frame. He wears a white suit. Wren makes the case to the photographer from channel six *Action News*. The photographer leaves the truck to wave his camera around the neighborhood, joking with Daryl, who stands to the side wearing a brown Fubu baseball shirt. Above, from the window factory's window, a couple of guys start to chant, *Hell no we won't go!* Later, when they file out of the broken-down, two-story warehouse, their bravado is gone. The factory owner has told them nothing. Even the book-keeper, an old-fashioned woman with bleached hair, silver make-up, and heavy black plastic earrings, is unsure of the plant's fate. Or at least so she says. *All I know is what the sign says*, pointing to the orange demolition notice. But out of cowardice, no one has filled in a date on the sign.

The demonstration grows. The neighbors fight for their wall, for their city. It *is* worth fighting for. I watch them stab handmade signs into the clear air. I listen to their voices. They shout for the city's immense soul, like preachers, to save it. Mark from Brooklyn, a ten-year transplant with a sugar-sweet smile and a mound of dreadlocks, strokes a thick metal tin drum, an *agogo* from Nigeria. An old black woman in gaudy pink pants has come to fight, as has a local cafe owner wearing a Spanish-style beard, and a young hippie couple carrying a sign: *Lies for Fries*. Larry's megaphone plays Old MacDonald, Old McDonald in our yard, ee, eye, ee, eye, oh! The protesters beckon horns from passing trucks. *Beat back the Mac attack! Not one resident wants it!*

13. THE INFINITE AND THE PAROCHIAL

AS the weather warms, old ladies in lawn chairs greet the sidewalk like children awakening on Christmas morning. Young girls ride back and forth on their Barbie bicycles. Heads pop out of windows and after months of quiet and early darkness, we hear voices stinging the street. In the purple and verdant white blooms of flower boxes are the seeds of people coming together. We hear music playing in an upstairs apartment and a rhythm re-emerging from deep inside the stone foundations. This is the social scene in the row house city, street after street, neighborhood to neighborhood. Conversation is constant. We crave each other, wait for each other.

There is a life to the stoop. Here we share the same arguments, the same stony silence, the games, and humor, the weather and gossip, sickness, medical advice, grandchildren, and casseroles, prom pictures, banjos, dominoes, dogs and cats, marigolds, brooms, bets, and stories. On stoops and porches, on the sidewalk's edge and the street corner, we are together, uninterrupted by time.

The banter goes on. It extends off the stoop and the corner, beyond the cans of Budweiser and the card table and the cards. The banter reaches corner stores and into cafes and bars and onto the bus, the park bench, the train station, the trolley car, the social club, the ball field, the dog run, the community garden, in the blaring light of the open day and the closed darkness of the night. Cities and neighborhoods are built for people to talk, to talk with each other and talk about themselves and their city.

The value of the parochial city is in the neighborhood banter. It is welcoming and confirming, like a warm bed at the close of the day. It is sweet comfort against the wind and familiar to the touch. We become a part of the banter, and we are therefore a part of something.

Twisted together on our feet and asses, we are joined together in the parochial city by simple geography. In this condition, we carry the extraordinary power of exclusion and denial, stratification and fear, as if there is a direct correlation between the worn stoop and hatred or lack of understanding. The longer we sit here, the deeper the groove and smoother the marble becomes. Our window to the world shrinks and eventually it closes, shade down, and in the vast city, we find ourselves alone.

It is easy to become trapped in the parochial city. The view from the stoop is short, expectations and encounters are limited. Perhaps we shorten the vista purposely. We turn the city into a village because we cannot contend with the infinite city. The soul of the city is so vast it is incomprehensible. Who can imagine an infinite number of lives, of hopes, of struggles? One block is enough to occupy our time. So we mettle. We worry. We sweep our sidewalk and hope others do the same.

All of us struggle to balance the comfort of the parochial city with the nourishment of the infinite. Some of us see the parochial city like a fortress. We plot our escape. This is the condition of the character Manela, an eighteen-year-old girl in the novel *War of the Saints* by Brazilian writer Jorge Amado. Manela lives with her Aunt Adalgisa on a tiny, mediocre street, the Avenida da Ave-Maria, in the reckless coastal city of Bahia. Adalgisa is strict and consequently Manela enjoys few freedoms. She is forced to live in her aunt's small, closed world. The war of the saints is a battle between the saints of the African Santeria, the saints of *Carnivale*, and the pious Catholic saints for control of Adalgisa's soul. The Santeria saints are fighting to free Manela from the binds of the dour, unloving parochial street. Adalgisa accepts only her regal Catholic, Andalusian heritage and ignores her other half, the African and Indian, the pagan.

During *Carnivale*, Manela escapes. In the heat of the festival, Manela meets a black man named Miro. He is there amidst the "horrible crush," dancing a *samba*. His teeth are bright, his skin dark, and his hair is a tall Afro. She cools Miro with sacred water from the washing ceremony and he liberates her. Amado says of Manela, "Overwhelmed by a feeling of relief, of well-being, the all-consuming urgent desire to live, an insidious euphoria, a sweet sadness, the liberated swallow flapped her wings, ready to take flight and discover the world." The black angel Miro has unlocked the gates of Manela's parochial life. She is but a princess in his arms. All of Bahia is hers.

Manela is about to experience for the first time the force of the infinite city, its endless humanity, its unguarded pain, its brilliant potential. Liberated from her aunt's small-minded grip, she falls at once into another world, amidst the fervor of an ancient, sensual celebration. Miro carries her across the city, past boundaries, eventually through walls she never even knew existed.

The infinite city is like the world itself. It is flat and wide and vast and in it everyone, everything can be known and explored, across cultures, and time and place. Relationships develop amidst the colossal realm of people from every corner of the globe. In the parochial city, Manela is forever trapped on the Avenida da Ave-Maria. She marries the man who Adalgisa chooses. But in the infinite city, she discovers Miro and crosses cultures. Her own African heritage awakens.

In the infinite city each person represents a culture, a home, an epic story, a journey. Each of us is plain spectacle for the rest to see and try to understand. This exchange of human knowledge can be simple and innocent. We spot a waiter and a waitress crowding the service door of a downtown restaurant for a smoke before their shift begins. We watch gregarious construction workers filling the early morning subway. We listen to a pair of old classmates who meet on the bus; they update each other and reminisce. They hug but neither makes an offer of a future encounter. Across the aisle laborers curse the boss. A little girl learns her colors on a park bench. A well-dressed man makes deals on his cell-phone sitting alone at the corner table of a café. We notice a new father at dawn, flowers in hand. Walking toward the hospital, he is exhausted and drained. But that wry smile is detectable, so clear even in the bleary hour. We smile back. Our faces stretch, our hearts expand. Each time, each small glimpse breaks down the complex. Now, I know you. Now, I know me.

A single person in the infinite city can be seen but also heard, her voice understood in spite even of herself, in spite of her own visions and paranoia. The grumpy, crazy woman who lives below us, who pokes the ceiling with a broom each time she imagines that we are dragging furniture across the floor, who writes us incomprehensible letters on forty-year-old stationery, the woman who we have never seen, is open to us. We hate her and curse her, we laugh, but in that handwriting, in the solemn and secure typeface at the top of the letter, she is there, alive.

Our relationship with the city stretches somewhere between the parochial and the infinite, between the Avenida da Ave-Maria and the whole of the Afro-Latin city of Bahia. Without either the city ceases to function. Take away the parochial and the remains are cold, commodified spaces where personal, local connections do not exist. There are no neighborhoods, no neighbors, just glances. Dismiss the infinite from the city and what's left is a village. The expectations are already known, the outcomes understood. The only way out is to leave.

We might consider again the story of the neighbors on Forty-third Street. In fighting to stop the McDonald's from being built, they are protecting their own block, their own homes. They have worked to make the block a comfortable place to live. For them it is a welcoming place, made even more desirable by the gardens they have created in the back. They value their parochial city. Yet it is not just the fate of their small block of South Forty-third Street that drives Wren Ingram mad with anger and has made Larry Falcon an anti-McDonald's crusader. They act because the city beckons them to stand up, to fight and win back its favor. They act because the back wall of their gardens is more than just a divider between properties. In a way it is a symbol of the infinite city. It is old, like the city itself. In the stucco and brick and mortar is the passage of time and people, infinite layers of desire and ambition. The wall awakens their spirits. They act because they know the McDonald's will deaden them. It will eviscerate their parochial life and the infinite city. In one sweep of the bulldozer, the idiotic clown will wreak havoc on their wall and destroy their beauty. This is their fear on Forty-third Street. They fight because they love the soul of the city, the soul that is at once a small village and the whole of the sensual world.

*

On July Fourth in Philadelphia, from inside a row house it feels like the city is under siege. Pop, seer, boom, boom, boom, thud. Billie Holiday plays on the radio and mixes with voices from a party out on the deck across the way. Outside, above the row houses and trees, past the skyscrapers and bridges dressed in red, white, and blue lights, across the flat horizon, all around I spot small displays. The fireworks are being tossed into the sky by kids and engineers, by sweating, beer-dribbling pyromaniacs. The sliver moon is trapped against the haze studded with green oblong balls, green, red, and silver swirls, white light ricocheting off the blue Ben Franklin Bridge. Way off in the distance in the macadam heat of the Vet parking lot and F.D.R. Park, tiny, personal shows are exploding all at once. This is the blood rite of independence. It is a special responsibility taken up by row-house boys in ribbed tank tops, black wispy mustaches, greasy long narrow sideburns, and dangling crosses.

It is twilight Independence Day 1999. The heat wave is already three weeks old. Harmon Zuckerman's Bronco pushes up Interstate 95, with the river and Camden on the right, the mess of river wards down below on either side of the highway. Traffic is light heading away from downtown. The road itself is littered with grit and shredded tires. He passes a billboard, silver, white, and blue, the Rocky Mountains. It says something about Philly being a Coors kind of town. He remembers, repeats for the thousandth time his father's adage: *the truth is always exactly the opposite of what the ad man says*. But he thinks of his raw, row-house city. Maybe this time they're right.

Off at Allegheny Avenue, the Bronco moves through Richmond. John Garfield once played a war hero from this section, blinded on the Tenaru River in hopeless fire with the Japs. He was a regular patriotic guy, a factory worker from Tulip Street and then a Marine. He fell in love with Eleanor Parker and saw her last on the platform at the Thirtieth Street Station.

Harmon takes the old Bronco down under the tracks of the Elevated. He is in the Barrio. The tracks that split Glenwood and Sedgley Avenues disrupt this mangled neighborhood even further. Two other lines cross right nearby. Streets dead end in wasteland. Mostly unused factories line the railroad. He passes a tannery, a furniture maker, twisted streets, a fire-charred Buick Century, a bar decorated with a tropical mural, the railroad trestle. On any day here the streets groan and crack. Girls in pink dresses and pigtails play in piles of rebar and slit marble under slanted ailanthus. *The tree of heaven*. A plastic bag drifts up in the heavy air and floats above a boy walking home. The corner is wrapped with young men. Others sit low in a red Camaro.

To get to Reese Street, he takes a right on Fifth, a quick left on Willard. Willard is not really a street at all, not much more than an empty alley. The land all around it is open and empty, brown. Fireworks and old-fashioned sparklers spray light from every direction and bottle rockets sizzle low to the ground. The drug dealers pay for the largest, most extravagant fireworks, but Reese Street has been waiting since the morning for their own show.

The street is decorated to be sure. Red, white, and blue flags hang from side to side. Latin music has been playing since seven in the morning. In the haze of dusk, children race around in excitement and parents drink beer. Harmon and Edward have come to Reese Street to help Jeff and Lisa, who live on the block, set off their show, to blow a grand in the blink of an eye. Straightforward community delight—this is their neighborly gift to Reese Street. For three-quarters of an hour, on a street no wider than a thumb, four white people perform for the Puerto Rican audience. Reese Street laughs and yells and holds its breath and clasps its children. The rocketry is fired rapidly and the spaces are tight. This show is given in the first person—it's right on top of you.

In a hurry, Harmon leaves the block party a few minutes after the show ends to make it to another party in Center City, to watch the annual display from a balcony just off the Parkway. Edward stays with Jeff and Lisa in the Barrio.

High off the street in the ancient blue-green Bronco, Harmon Zuckerman bounces through the ghetto like Klinger in a garden dress driving a jeep across a minefield. He bumps and dodges. He crosses Broad Street at Lehigh, and in the steel and vinyl chamber with all the windows open, the air is hot and thick. North Philadelphia is blurry, rupturing. Harmon is uncustomarily uncomfortable.

He works the Bronco down Fifteenth Street and jumps over to Parrish thinking that he will park around Fairmount Avenue and walk to the party. But at Parrish the familiar, reliable street grid turns, then it turns again. Harmon finds himself caught in an isosceles triangle formed by two smaller triangles at ninety-degree angles to each other. At the edge of the triangle are signs of disaster and decay and a neighborhood he never knew existed.

Then traffic stops. Ahead of him and behind him, drivers abandon their cars and run down to Fairmount Avenue to catch the fireworks display. The street tumbles ahead of him. Hundreds of people smother the sidewalks and the center of the avenue. Traffic is stopped for a reason. On the Fourth of July, Philadelphia is carnival and motion. This is the day the city celebrates its saints.

Sitting on top of the Bronco's bubble hood, Harmon watches with the driver of the car behind him. The hot steel stings their legs. They can't see much of anything—only the very highest and brightest can be spotted up above the brownstones and belfries. When the show is over, the night is dark again. Headlights sweep the street and street lamps illuminate people heading in every direction.

Harmon is amazed by the street scene but still uncomfortable. He is anxious to leave. He wants to make it to the party. At every turn he finds an obstacle. A shirtless eleven-year-old charges him a dollar to drive through a vacant lot. A cop stops him from crossing the Parkway. Harmon ignores the boy, lies to the cop, and says he is trying to get home. A few minutes later, he sits on the balcony of an apartment building, overlooking the scene. Up here, he finds relief from the carnival. A breeze awakens the dense air. Up here he sits above a massive asphalt parking lot. The city spreads north and west before him. He passes the night making bets on which car will be the last to leave the parking lot.

*

The streets of the city seem to go on infinitely in confounding uniformity, and at times in a rousing variety. The Bronco, like a big-eared bad ass in a black hat, barrels through the streets. For those inside the truck, it is never a comfortable ride. This Ford, one of the first mass-produced trucks designed for bare bones fishing trips, to haul a boat or a slaughtered deer, moves like a stagecoach crossing the Nebraska hills. It takes the pitted streets of Philadelphia and the cobblestones and the trolley tracks, but the street takes the Bronco and eats it up, swallows it, and tosses it back out. Over and over again. The vehicle looks, incidentally, like a direct descendent of the Tin Lizzy; only no one with a Model T ever grew an aloe plant on the floor behind the driver's seat.

A flat Kelly green covers the fenders, setting off the sapphire blue body and the faded pink horses on the wheels. In spots the paint is chipped clear to the metal. The spare tire cover is ripped, the vinyl dash cracked to the orange foam. The foam smells like a cold morning, like hot coffee and cigarettes and breath brown as leather. Before she died, Grandmama liked the Bronco best. After her stroke, she lost her independence, but not, apparently, her sense. She preferred him to take her out in the old truck rather than in her own Acura. That way Harmon had to lift her up and into the passenger seat. She liked the closeness and his strength and being lifted up high above the street.

Harmon stands at average height, his black hair is thick and heavy, untamable. Only Murray's hair oil, which is available in African American neighborhoods, can tame this Jewish mane. The oil holds his hair down but thickens it all the same. He occasionally shaves it clean or cuts it short, keeping or cutting the sideburns, growing or shaving the goatee or just the beard, once or twice leaving the hair long, the sideburns ample, and otherwise just a mustache—so that he might resemble a character in a Paul Schrader film.

He likes things hard. He prefers extremes and possibilities and danger. He seeks difference in people, in his daily routine, in his beliefs. He is at once hypocritical and perfectly consistent, and either position suits him anyway. Lunch with Grandmama one moment, the next he is screwing a fitness instructor named for a type of cheese. Then he's off to play three sets of tennis, to watch his little sisters, or he stops at one or two or three friends' houses. He works on his Ducati motorcycle or the truck, hits the 700 Club or the Standard Tap, plays the guitar, and he talks. His shirt is tight, the sleeves clinging hard to his biceps. He talks and whomever he is talking to, at that moment, has all of his attention. He lives every single moment of life at a constant and consistent energy, like a hard rain. But the rain might stop at any moment and Harmon Zuckerman will be gone, and the red Ducati Super Sport off to someplace else in the vast, flat city.

Philadelphia is and always will be Harmon's world. If he leaves it, and he has several times in his thirty or so years, he will return and he will still find wonder in its people, in the streets and neighborhoods where he has walked a thousand times. He is drawn by his own father's devotion to the city and his father himself and by Grandmama. Through his pale green eyes, he sees himself at the top of a mystical mountain and that mountain is Philadelphia. He sees himself again and he is the mountain. Harmon appears to be unobligingly indiscernible from the city. He cannot be pried free.

Yet he is obsessed by the whole of the material world, by geology, which he studied in college, by cities everywhere, by buildings and architecture, by food, by the force of the landscape, by motorcycle engines, by wine and beer and scotch and coffee.

These obsessions will never pass. Harmon is the son of a college professor, and he has spent a quarter of a lifetime with his father, his affable and unsparingly accepting father, debating and discussing ideas of every measure. Together, they possess the sugar man's way of analyzing the world, of concluding oceans from the spotting of a stream and doing so generously, almost lovingly. Not only can Harmon or Mike Zuckerman spot an ocean from its source, but when they describe it, it is a deep magnetic blue, a blue the sky can never obtain.

Harmon stays up late into the night reading Naomi Wolf or Ian McHarg, whom he idolizes, or Steinbeck. He listens forthrightly to Roosevelt's great speeches. He can recite them from memory. Harmon dreams of a contemporary New Deal. He is a thinker, a social critic, an idealist who spends hours scanning the Ducati chat group on-line, fixing the Bronco's fuel line, playing poker in Brooklyn, playing guitar with someone's uncle on a side street in Frankford, driving cross-country with an old friend, thinking about Allen Iverson and Steve Carlton, John Lee Hooker and the Rolling Stones, reviewing the previous day's box scores, pledging to give up altogether on the Phillies and realizing that to do so would be like ending a long and mutually dependent marriage.

Harmon's life is like a great, flat open plain. And that plain is Philadelphia. He spreads himself across the open plain, down the alleys and into the corner bars, along the river. The city is like his old, wise teacher. It has seen it all, felt every emotion. Here is Harmon, listening to the teacher and searching, learning, and repeating. It is not enough for him to see something once, to talk to someone once, to hang out somewhere once, but he must do it again across time. His understanding and uncommon perception come in the repetition. See and do something once at six years old and again across the span of a life—across the span of a city—and the vision becomes sharper. The stream is alive with fish and algae, molecules and cells, but only appears that way on the sixth or eighth sighting. The stream becomes an ocean unto itself. Each time Harmon spreads himself a little further in his city or reverts back to an old and comfortable place, a part of him uncoils and he is somehow, desperately more alive. The open plain of his life is thickening with details and experience—grass to meadow to forest.

Harmon met Edward in preschool at Nineteenth and Christian, at the St. Charles Church Montessori School. As Harmon remembers it, the headmaster was a Belgian priest who was color-blind. The priest taught them long division at three years old. The school was where Harmon learned the colors of the city. He was living at the time in a small house on a park at the edge of an Irish working-class neighborhood. The much older, angry kids, the kids in the gangs fighting over streets and territory, were all white. But Nineteenth and Christian, which was no more than ten blocks away from his house, was a black neighborhood, and the other children in his school were black. There he was at three, already extending himself into the city, beyond his Jewish house and his Irish neighborhood and into a Catholic church on a bright, wide, handsome street in black South Philly, near the street where the great soprano Marian Anderson was raised, in the neighborhood where he now lives.

Down on the grassy, overgrown side of the river, the east bank of the Schuylkill, where garbage is tossed and left as a matter of course, he and Edward would smoke cigarettes and shoot squirrels with BB guns. They also had a bow and arrow and wrist rockets to nail pigeons and rats. With the city all around them, they would explore some measure of untamed wilderness. This was before the pretty park at Spruce Street and the concrete bridge at Walnut. Edward became an auto mechanic, opening his own shop at Fifteenth and Fairmount. But then he was just a lanky kid, tall as a post and no wider, from a W.A.S.P. family on the skids. His mother was a scholar of classic Latin and Greek. Edward might have been reciting the Aeneid in Greek as they climbed along the rickety footbridge under the Walnut Street Bridge, but Harmon can't be sure.

He does remember looking down below the bridge, with cars crossing back and forth above their heads, and seeing men fucking in the
grass. The riverside is not called Judy Garland Park for nothing.

At nine, he was responsible for walking Maria, his little sister, to
preschool. She relished his attention and he loved to take her
through the alleys and carriage house blocks and down Delancey,
past stone mansions. Already, these were his streets. On bike,
Harmon found himself able to reach the playground way out on
Haverford Avenue in West Philly, the Wissahickon Skating Club in
Chestnut Hill, the ball fields on the Parkway, and a friend's house in
Mount Airy. He began to understand the place where he lived. Like
every school kid in the city, he lived on buses, subways, and trains.
Since he attended Central High School, a magnet school, his friends
were scattered across the plain, in South Philly and North Central
and Overbrook and West Philadelphia and Fairmount and Oak Lane
and Germantown and Oxford Circle, Frankford, Torresdale,
Wissanoming and the Far Northeast. But Harmon's friends were
not just his classmates. He has always befriended older people,
people he has learned from, whose lives he has entered. Those
Harmon found were men usually, like Al from Manayunk who
looked over all of them in high school; Jack, the homeless man from
Hurricane, West Virginia, who lived on the bank of the Schuylkill;
Gim Sik the Korean skater; Frank Cornstalk, the alcoholic Native
American carpenter; John the banker; Bruce who sells antiques;
and Sid, who made an extraordinary film about Vietnam Veterans.

Everyday he sees them. They are there, like personal historic
markers, reminders. Sometimes he sees a street or a building that
reminds him of someone, and he stands and looks and weeps.
There is Christian, a new friend from Fishtown who hangs out at
the Standard Tap and plays softball on Sundays. Christian is in his
early twenties. He likes to stay out all night, play guitar, and smoke.
This makes Harmon feel sixteen again. He feels the excitement and

danger he felt then. Even now, he still hears the gun fire on Berkley Street in Germantown. He sees the neighborhood kids storming the house like the A.T.F., and the punk kids, who squatted in vacant buildings all over the city, playing music. He sees himself go back in to grab a friend, whose name he does not remember. In the brazen silence of the New Year's morning they piled into Al's Plymouth Valiant station wagon and reversed down the street at forty miles an hour, the shots ringing Wayne Avenue. Somehow, magically, they crossed the valley and came to Manayunk. They spotted a woman stumbling down Pechin Street, blood circling her legs. She was naked as the year began. They brought her into the station wagon. She would not, could not speak. Her voice had been taken by the rape, and she was left abandoned. At that moment it was over. They spent the morning covering the ruined city in the car and trying to get the woman to talk, to find out where she lived, to help her. The morning vanished and Harmon found his way home. He doesn't remember how.

Harmon bought his first motorcycle at fifteen. They called it the Moto Guizzi Custom Cruiser, the "spaghetti Harley"; it was big and somewhat slow and ideal for long distance travel. The red 1994 Ducati that he purchased later is fast and uncomfortable. The sound of its engine is a guttural call that only a select few can hear and understand. In the city, where he needs only his feet and a subway or bus token to get around, a couple bucks here or there for a cab, he keeps two impractical vehicles.

The Bronco is a $750 project, a hobby, and wherever he goes it commands a ridiculous, hard American respect. The truck is big and ugly, a twenty-five-year-old cultural icon that no one will steal, that no one will mess with, that made his Grandmama giggle. He relishes driving it while wearing a suit and talking on his cell phone, toying with the sodden expectations of anyone else on the road. But in the Bronco, it is easiest to picture Harmon Zuckerman, unfiltered

Camel and phone at his mouth, crossing his own great plain, simultaneously back through the layers of his singular existence and out into the unknown, the infinite city of his own creation.

There he is with his father—and still to this day—standing outside at ten in the evening waiting in line at Italio's Water Ice at Twelfth and Shunk or at Nick's Roast Beef at Twentieth and Jackson. He's ordering lamb chops at Wolf's Butcher on Baltimore Avenue or eating a Sid and Fran Special at Koch's Deli on Locust. There is Harmon Zuckerman walking to Hebrew School at Society Hill Synagogue and at a party in the house of a man who owned a bar named Bacchanal and in Edward's garage at three in the morning fixing the Ducati. And he is there in the Central High Locker Office with Steve and Matt and in Matt's house on Webster Street and helping Matt lay pavers on someone's sidewalk. And there he is with Niovi and Pablo and the rest of Greek Philadelphia at Laurie's café, making dinner for all the customers. At four in the morning he's being let back into Doobies for a few more drinks and the gentle end to the day. Some have left Harmon's city. But each of them is still here, in the streets and the uneven brick sidewalks, and they will be here until Harmon has lost his mind or his capacity to see and remember.

At times, though, this world seems to recoil around him. It moves him to see the same people around the bar at the 700 Club, to play softball every week with the whole crowd from the Northern Liberties, with Bernadette and Richard and Seth and Iva and Chris and Rachel and Owen and Michelle and Jon Rossi and little Gabor and Brad and Nancy. While he does not live in the Liberties, it has become his adopted home. Occasionally, he has been caught in the midst of a local Liberties drama, of braised loved, of fire bombings, of restlessness and easy sex. And then the Bronco hits the road. He seeks some kind of difference, variety in the landscape. When this world shrinks, becomes too suffocating and parochial, he plays the city's tightrope back towards the infinite

and the unknown; he seeks the perfect tension. Unlike the character Manela, who is either trapped by the parochial city or liberated
in the infinite possibilities of *Carnivale*, Harmon chooses both. Both
are his Philadelphia. He embraces the soul of Philadelphia while sitting at the intimate bar of the 700 Club, talking for hours to people
he sees everyday. He encounters the soul of Philadelphia while having a beer with Jeff's neighbors on Reese Street in the Barrio, while
setting up the fireworks show, while watching the faces of the children on the block as they race around oblivious to the July humidity. There are parts of the city, like the Barrio, that he doesn't know
well and going there is adventure, release, and uncertainty. Manela
was liberated from the parochial city, but even in Miro's arms she
must have been frightened. The infinite city can be unnerving, on
the day of carnival or not.

*

The Independence Day 2000 party on Reese Street is better organized than it was the year before. This time, the street is roped off at
either end and two boxes of fireworks are already set out, a main
show and a finale. Edward brought his Goth friends, and they all
watch Jeff and Lisa set up. They have arranged a series of bottle
rockets to start the show. As Lisa lights the first, the tube twists,
and the rocket shoots low and fast, nearly hitting a small boy.
Before she can catch the second one, the misadventure happens
again and the rocket appears to be aimed at another child. But
someone pushes the five-year-old out of the way and the rocket
drills the chain-link fence instead.

Harmon thinks he has a solution to the twisting tube and he
starts to fix the problem. But Jeff stops him. Jeff has lived here on
Reese Street all his life, inheriting the house from his parents. He
and Lisa are the only non-Puerto Ricans on the block, and they are
trusted as good neighbors. The fireworks show is part of building

that trust. If they ignore the danger to the children and push on, they risk disturbing the trust. They do not want to even appear to have been insensitive. All of this Jeff communicates to Harmon with the wave of a sweaty hand, a simple gesture. *Take the bottle rockets away.*

It is then that the world around Harmon stops. He notices the pause, an uncomfortable silence. On the tiny block with the carnival blasting all around he is given a lesson on the politics of the street, on the rules that govern a cramped, diverse place. This is Philadelphia's greatest value, he thinks, pushing so many different people side-by-side, and sometimes it works. Just now, the rules worked and Jeff understood them. And he, Harmon, for a moment, did not.

Disaster having been narrowly averted, Jeff continues the show. He lights four thousand individual firecrackers, one called the Pit Bull. At the end the neighbors give him a standing ovation. This time Jeff and Lisa, Harmon, Edward, and the Goth friends all leave the Barrio, determined to see the city's show on the Parkway. Wanting to avoid getting caught in a maelstrom of people, Harmon cuts a wide path to Center City. The route is fast and they step on to the Parkway at Twenty-third Street just as the show begins. Hundreds of thousands of others stand there too, the humidity having only increased. Here is Harmon's city of difference, all together, sweating.

Back toward home, Harmon stops at the 700 Club. Everyone is there to greet him with hugs and two-cheek kisses. The small pale green room is filled, and he knows everyone. Perhaps they have been here since softball ended or perhaps not, but he suspects, he knows, few of them ever leave the Northern Liberties. The neighborhood is that comfortable. He rests in this comfort and talks baseball for a while. He knows, too, that his night will not end here in the warm embrace of the 700 Club. Harmon will continue on. He won't sleep until most are rising. But the next day, at some point, he might return.

14. DARKNESS

IT'S dark, the air fragrant and cool. The street commands a late-night silence disturbed only by sirens and occasional foot play on the pavement. The neon yellow of storefront windows cuts through the darkness. Well past midnight a wind stirs. Men in jeans, hands stuffed in their pockets, fill a vestibule. A couple walks slowly home. Up above and out over the entrenched street, out through the formal windows of a once-decadent mansion, I hear a DJ's scarring and incessant beat. A small crowd shuffles through a wide-open doorway.

Night is the darkness of the city's soul. The darkness is not, as we might characterize a person's soul, a measure of evil or terror. Of course, evil and intrigue thrive in the night city. Police cars race down empty avenues. Knives are pulled. Tricks are played. Love is sold. But many of us don't fear the night. Rather, the darkness releases us from the constraints of the day. It is a time of freedom and opportunity, of abandon. The darkness protects us. Shadows hide us. We mask ourselves in the night.

In the morning we find bottles in the gutter, drug baggies, and condoms. Through these things we think we understand the night. But anything, everything happens in the night city. In the day, the street energy is diffused. We are wound in the day's work, each of us like a bee, buzzing around, pollinating or making honey. At night the street energy is concentrated in the darkness. It pushes us forward, making us brazen. We become the person we'd never dare be in the day. We strip, safe in the darkness. We exchange clothes, body parts, partners. All the while we realize that the night street has the quality of a stage. It is lit only to emphasize the scene. Otherwise the house is dark. And we perform.

*

I climb the stairs of the old mansion and step into a bright room. The room is full already, though the ball hasn't started. Those who came early sit in folding metal chairs arranged in a horseshoe, with tables for the judges and the commentator at the open end. The commentator has the crowd's attention. He speaks rapidly. He rhymes. He talks to the beat. Some hold video cameras and others pace around ready to walk up the runway. A few sit in chairs, watching, cheering, just to stretch the night into morning. Sometime after one in the morning, the commentator introduces the host family of the ball, the House of Karan. He calls each person individually, like at the start of a basketball game. He lauds them. Individually, they prance to the front. They are gay, bi, transsexual, transvestite, whatever, and all African American. The loudest cheers are for the tall, full-breasted transsexuals, the femme queens. Each member of the House of Karan delivers a warning statement on A.I.D.S. Their language is direct. They repeat percentages from memory. It is a public service. At the end of the introductions, while the commentator introduces the judges, the members group together for a photo. The judge's table is filled with legends, old-timers, the "mothers" and "fathers" of all of those gathered in the room.

We slouch quietly in the disarray before the show. The room is a knot of bodies. At last the commentator calls for femme queens to show "face." They compete for beauty. The judges decide who has the most gorgeous complexion. A femme queen appears from the crowd of long tender men and others bent over in their chairs, bored, as if watching a school awards ceremony. If she looks good, like a real girl, and she shows her stuff to the judges and if we would never know to pass her on the street—like the ads say at the back of the paper—"with a pretty little secret," she might face a challenger—a thick woman in leather, a black cowgirl. The two contestants face off in the center of the room on the second floor, and the judges rank them accordingly.

I find Qiyammah Rashid among the crowd in the warm room. Tonight she won't walk the runway. The DJ's music grinds a continuous stop and go, repeating, and the heat in the room rises, our faces becoming flush. The energy circles the runway. It rises up out of the crowd. It's like Sunday morning in a black storefront church, a la James Baldwin. The open vogue competition throws bodies on the floor and arms in the air, hollering. So many sexual references and so many swollen manufactured breasts. Butch girls walk the floor and turn to face the judges. Each might well have been a man, or an outcast boy at least. But only one gets a trophy. Some have come in from New York or Baltimore for a chance. As the commentator drones on, the femme queens steal the show. They shake the room with dark two-way allure, beloved like goddesses, their hideous beauty a late Friday night revelation.

*

Qiyammah Rashid stands outside her grandmother's door on Lena Street in Germantown. She's just getting up for the day, though it is already past noon. She stayed out late, until the stars began to disappear in the earliest light. Her grandmother doesn't know where she goes so late at night or what the trophies are for—though she thinks there must be something queer about it. But she doesn't hold her back or tell her not to go.

The sun is milky bright, the glare heavy. The porch is shady. Every porch on the south side of Lena Street is connected and each is painted a bright color. As I stand on the porch I see a rainbow above—green, pink, gray, yellow, peach, and orange—as I look down the block. Across the way, the houses are decorated with Moorish details. The rooflines are so curvy they seem to dance. Porches drip with petunia and hosta, lobelia, portulaca, and marigolds, plastic pansies and jasmine. The air smells of trash and mulch, of hedges mostly trimmed. This is a solid and proud block, where pension checks are spent on home equity loans. Every Saturday the ladies hold "café." They drink iced tea, eat sandwiches, and sit at round tables listening to Harry Belafonte.

Qiyammah is like the Princess of Germantown. She wears a low-cut chambray skirt and white heels. Her enormous chest out in front, she heads toward Germantown Avenue. At the corner she hands her cousin, who is sixteen and just coming out, a couple of dollars for toothpaste and deodorant. We continue down Coulter, the whistles following Qiyammah like a bad stench, but she's used to it. She *knows* she is beautiful.

At sixteen Qiyammah had seen enough of the straight club scene, the groping and grinding. She liked to dress *hot,* to show a little *extra.* The men, the straight men, could not handle it. So she switched to gay bars and clubs, where she encountered no *drama,* where she could dance unhampered by sexual aggression and everyone in the crowd adored her. Late at night in the clubs, she learned other roles. She encountered new possibilities. *I just act like a damn faggot,* she repeats in her nasal-stuffed voice, the words pouring out in a kind of ghetto mumble. Qiyammah smiles her giant smile, knowing she is funny and irreverent and more confident than a Texas oilman at a political rally. Her face is long, her nose narrow. She sucks on the silver ball tongue ring in her mouth. She sticks it out for additional emphasis, breathes in, sticks it out again, drops her hands by her side and sighs.

She met Alvernian, Father Prestige, at a club on Thirteenth Street. Father saw trophies, a straight girl who needed care. He saw someone who could walk face *and* body. She must have shocked him with her straightforward intensity. But she was looking too, seeking some kind of shelter, some kind of love, an easier way to survive the phony days and the long violent nights.

The House has gone through upheaval and is down to twelve family members. A few had to be tossed. They were not serious enough about Prestige, but here they are in the glossy photograph, shiny black angels in arctic white, or in silver, industrial, painted faces and dyed hair, before the grand march at the start of the ball. But the photos are a mirage, a trick of identity. What seems to be there is really absent. Or it is there. It all depends on what is real.

In the infinite universe of sexual identity, gender, and transgressions, of chromosomes and accidents, of playfulness and experimentation, of danger and exploitation, of ideal beauty and Hollywood grandeur, of a wispy Anglo-Francophile homosexuality, of a great tossed salad of *européenne* cultural iconography, is the House of Prestige. And the House of Mizrachi, the House of Gucci, of Ebony, Karan, Blanik, and Excellence. They are royal houses and fashion houses and sorority houses, and 1950s perfect families, each idealized, dramatized, picked apart, and mixed together with all the assuredness, pluck, and boisterous awareness of the postmodern world.

The House of Prestige, with its twelve members, is comparatively small. Of course Father Prestige is a legend so he has little to prove by raising a large family. Other houses support fifty, eighty family members. Some are predominantly white, Asian, Latino, whatever. They are shelter and belonging for all kinds of gays and lesbians, transsexuals and transvestites. Each house contains a small, parochial world, a comfortable place to come out or not, to pretend or not, to switch identity, and forget the sweat and shivers of the daytime lie. But the comfort, the ease of the house, and the hidden world of the late night balls is itself liberty, freedom to assume a life, and live it. The night city shelters them just as the body of the city harbors immigrants. They crave the vast darkness— where there are no judgmental grandmothers or belligerent, bored friends from the neighborhood or even husbands and wives. The freedom of the night city is an unshackled search for honesty and openness and in the middle of a runway with cameras flashing, an encounter with true identity.

Qiyammah became the Princess of the House of Prestige, which endowed her with the responsibility of mentoring and looking after other family members, of deciding house policies, accepting or rejecting applicants, and tossing members, too. Her four or five trophies made her royalty. So she joined the rest of the royal family on the board of the House. Here is Qiyammah in Father's House in West Philadelphia, just two blocks from Nilien Insurance and Benkady Fatima Restaurant, but miles from proprietary Lena Street and the rose bush climbing up and over the trellis. In the House of Prestige, and in the long nights at the clubs and the balls, Qiyammah is free. This bizarre universe is hers.

Our Princess is treated accordingly, with respect and jealousy. They respect her, they all do, the butch girls and the butch queens, the femme queens and the real girls and the drag queens and the trade guys. Qiyammah Rashid is herself, a woman. She is a woman about to start college. She has survived the streets with one brother dead and another paralyzed. Her mother is dead too. And she wants to hang out with *them*. Most of them are part of the House because they had never belonged anywhere else. Qiyammah is their Princess and she loves them.

The members of the House of Prestige meet on an overgrown street with summer weeds in every crack. Here is this girl who wears her hair down to her damn ass if she feels like it. Here in the House of Prestige, they are to be themselves too, never mind what is between the legs. Turn a man into a woman each day and the pain is brutal. Qiyammah may keep a closet full of wigs, but she needs no hormonal shots to look pretty. For this the femme queens despise her. All the expense and inner rage. Woman inside of man, a trick of fate.

To Qiyammah the whole crowd can get downright Judy, especially at the balls. They think they are better than you, or whiter, which might be the same thing. They think they have worked harder for it, overcome more. What about you, real girl, do you have razor burn and stubble bumps? What about you? Do you defy nature to be beautiful and glamorous? It is all about that after all, fashion and competition, equating outside beauty to inner peace. But theirs is no different from the world they are imitating.

The balls are corny and fun as much as they are serious competition. Win for being convincingly handsome or looking like a real man or being really well dressed, for the fit of your Italian suit. Win a trophy for being chosen the First Lady of Face. *You are married to the leader of this great nation. Represent him in the right way.* Or try this: *It's fall and the cotton has to be picked. Some slaves have to be chained and some were glad to be houseboys.*

At a ball, identity, unfurled, is sent out to the floor. It is like a gathering of superegos with X-ray vision. Everyone has license to be whatever and everyone else *knows*. Even the trade guys are there, giving it or taking it in the bathroom, denying it out on the street. In all the fakery and the ludicrous grasping of glamorous royalty, in all the pretending, the borrowed clothes and the makeup, is a sharing. In a rented hall on Thirteenth Street, in the intimidating deepest dark of night it happens, this uncommon openness.

We're all a big ass family, repeats Qiyammah the Princess. She is thinking about much more than the House of Prestige. She pictures all of Thirteenth Street and the nighttime rituals. Qiyammah is accepted there though she is straight. She goes, not for the sexual promise of the night, but in spite of it. So she watches everyone else. Every week, she sees the same familiar figures in the dark. She spots the new faces in an instant. Realizing that she might come to know them in some particular clarity, she reaches for them like a mother. The journey into the night city is so often long, so brutally long.

FOUR: SEED

15. TOIL AND AN ACT OF FAITH

WE know from biblical text and ancient history that the kings of Babylonia and Persia mellowed and eventually allowed the Jews to return to Jerusalem. We learn that God forgave the city for its sins and commanded that the east gate be sealed forever. We hear from an anonymous prophet on the occasion who declares (Isaiah: 52:1), "Awake, awake put on your strength, O Zion; put on your beautiful garments, O Jerusalem, the holy city; for there shall no more come into you the uncircumcised and the unclean. Shake yourself from the dust, arise, O captive Jerusalem; loose the bonds from your neck, O captive daughter of Zion." We can imagine the people returning to their city, their princess. In their eyes after so many years she must have appeared even more beautiful than before she was destroyed. How they must have wept, grateful for their return.

The returning Jews cast new seed into the hills of Judea so that their princess might be reborn. Their seed was toil to be sure, and, incidentally, monetary aid from Persia too. They toiled with their hands, with a fierceness and pride. Their city would, after all, represent them and their beliefs, and of course their God. They rebuilt the city's body, the altar first, then the walls and houses. They re-sanctified Jerusalem, cleansed her soul as commanded by their God. By returning to the task of living and dying within her walls, they set her breathing deeper. The reclamation of Jerusalem was an historic event. The seed of the repatriated Jews took firm hold in the loose, dry soil. *Their* Jerusalem grew alongside the holy grounds of the old palace of David. It grew from their seed for two hundred years or more—until the Greeks came and cast their own seed, and Jerusalem changed once again.

The history of Jerusalem is like this. The seed of one tribe follows that of another. Roots take hold, but from the perspective of history they are ephemeral. They are easily disturbed in the shallow desert. Each of us city dwellers is like an epoch in the history of Jerusalem. Just by breathing the air and walking the streets of the city, we cast our seed here. The seed takes hold, over and over and the city changes. Eventually we die, move, or give up.

Just as plants use bees to carry seed, to pollinate and regenerate, the city uses us. The city trusts us to carry it forward through time. (Such blind faith might be dangerous—the city does not account for taste or values.) We oblige the city's need to regenerate, and to survive. In turn we use the city as a stage, a canvass, or playground. Certainly some seeds are stronger than others, but in our city no one person commands the terrain, not one particular group, or one God. Our city is truly filled with disparate voices. The seed is dispersed by so many.

There are times when disparate voices join together to fight for something, as the neighbors on Forty-third Street are organizing against the McDonald's. There are times when people from every corner of the city come together to support or oppose a change in the schools or in the government. In these cases, seeds are cast in unison, and they carry more weight than those tossed by each individual alone. For an observer of the cityscape, mass movements are spectacular to watch. People working together create a life energy that is far greater than the sum of each person's seed. Often, like the repatriating Jews, they believe their task is holy, of singular importance. Spreading seed is orgasmic, wholly lacking perspective. It is an act of narrow force, euphoria, righteousness, and greed. The group energy and the sanctity of the act make the toil that much easier and the impact that much stronger. The roots that grow from a group's seeds are short lived nevertheless (surely any nation that has tried to conquer Jerusalem understands this), but they spread deeply even in wasteland.

*

The spring they started to work, they found the soil to be gray not brown, and lifeless as if fallout from a nuclear accident. It would have been a lie to say that the ground was made from soil. Pulverized rebar, concrete, and brick would be more accurate. The land stretches for two acres out from the bakery and down to the hulking silent brewery and the forgotten cobblestone street. A dissection of that scarred earth would have shown perhaps, only microscopic life forms, but not a living worm or a red ant. The soil might have taken fifty years to regenerate on its own, to thrust itself back to life, to generate something more than dust and grievous reminders of the past. Still, a group of neighbors looked on the ground, long contested and appropriated—where hundreds of thousands of dollars had already been spent in plans and bulldozers, where thousands of men and women had worked, where a creek called Cohochsink once flowed and hides were beaten, where Tuscarora rice was milled and record albums were pressed—and they saw barrenness but also an opportunity for growth and for green. Other factions in the neighborhood saw something else. Years before, plans had been made to renovate the old tannery for apartments and many in the neighborhood, even after the buildings had been demolished, clung to the idea of development.

The volunteers stood looking at their scrubby, insatiable earth and at the purple, aquamarine, and white tourist carriages, one by one heading south. Hands in gloves and gloves on shovels, they faced lost days, doubt, and government forms. They hoped to find reasons and motivation for living, not alone but tangled amidst a web of others. Their goal was to build a garden on the land. They followed their instincts, the path of small money, and the convincing power of creative voices. After watching others working the rough, deceased earth, new bodies joined out of curiosity. And always, for three years at least, the questions and doubt hung over their toil. Would the other neighborhood factions stop pushing for something else besides a green fertile square, for something more valuable to bankers and real estate brokers? Would the city itself absorb the mountainous cost of the demolition of the buildings that once stood on the parcel or would the half a million dollars suffocate the project and eventually destroy it, turning it back to those who only wished to build? So they campaigned for their position while the Saturdays and Sundays rolled by and workdays extended well into summer nights. A few quiet ones like Luther, whose ancestors were Delaware farmers, couldn't stop. Once the hoe was in the ground, it was near impossible to pull it out and go home.

*

Jesse Gardner has the eyes of a true believer. They are blue and close set. His complexion is light, his personality strong. Jesse's Ukrainian grandparents were peddlers who made artificial flowers. He is a wheelwright and a carriage maker, a landscape architect, a painter of rough and harrowing cityscapes. His paintings are dense, the brushstrokes thick and impressionistic, full of shadows and orchestrated light and musty, muted yellow air. He insisted the neighbors act quickly, ignore rules and political protocol so that the city would not take back the parcel. Plant substantial trees first. What politician would bulldoze a tree?

He carefully chose the crab apple, red maple, hawthorne, locust, willow oak, and linden that would line the common. Jesse is a perfectionist and an entrepreneurial crusader. He is something of a combination of his meticulous Episcopalian ancestry—his grandfather was a senator in the New Jersey legislature—and the hardscrabble merchants from the Ukraine. His parents measure this tension. They are far right-wingers who not that long ago were sure-fire socialists. Jesse foots this balance, consciously. Gregarious and driven, in short order Jesse Gardner became the pulsing two-tone of the Liberty Lands. Eventually he pushed, like a massive uterine heave, a new pasture into being.

But none of the neighbors who cast the seed of Liberty Lands were there at the project's start, when Northern Liberties neighborhood leaders proposed to develop the tannery, a ponderous collection of three-, four-, and five-story industrial buildings, into housing. The idea for the park was conceived later, after the development plans failed and the buildings were torn down. When Dennis Haugh saw the fallen buildings and the immense rubble, he had a vision for a park. Quickly he began to gather support for the proposal. Dennis claims that it was only because of the success of the first Northern Liberties Days, when neighbors constructed a volleyball net from used plastic bags and Fifth Street was closed to cars and made human again, that he saw the power in local, collective action.

It had already been a year since the tannery just west of Second Street was demolished, the lot standing frozen and smothered in bricks and tires, when Dennis joined the board of the neighborhood association. He proposed to the group that the parcel be used by the neighborhood for gardening and recreation, and for a farmer's market, until a suitable development could be executed. But anyone who knows Dennis or has seen his decorative paintings and murals understands that his head is filled with trees and birds and insects and bright, warm summer sun. His vision for the parcel was not detached but surreal. Though his demeanor is quiet, the idea of the Liberty Lands burned inside him. Despite his conviction, the prodevelopment side of the board rejected his proposal.

Dennis moved ahead with the project. He uncovered enough funding to push forward, to make the initiative official. As the development faction of the board redoubled efforts to stop the project, he asked Jesse to draw up a plan. The source of funding was the

Philadelphia Urban Resources Partnership, a project of the U.S. Agriculture Department designed to help small communities enhance their environment, to remediate industrial soil, and plant community gardens. P.U.R.P., as the program is called, offered the Northern Liberties $59,000 in support to build the Liberty Lands. The neighborhood association was required to match the grant through volunteer hours and in-kind donations of plant materials and equipment. The immediate promise of funding forced the board to relent and allow the project to start. Most importantly, the grant enabled community members to hire a professional from outside the neighborhood to steer the complex project of building a park from dead ground and rubble. Jesse Gardner had only one choice. He stared ahead like a pitcher on the mound and dug in.

All the while Jesse continued interior and exterior landscaping at the airport and painting, from which he derived half his income. He courted his landlord's niece who is Chinese and was living in Beijing. She hosted him on a visit there and they become engaged as he left her side to return to Philadelphia. The newly affianced became pen pals, her aunt translating the letters. He worked upstairs in an enormous loft at the top of one of the most handsome buildings in all of Chinatown.

The first days they worked like peasants, twenty or sixty of them at a time, working by hand and back and pick axe and hoe. They resisted the land to break it, hauling televisions and tires and rebar and great inexhaustibly heavy chunks of concrete and marble. The wet weekends of that spring seemed endless, the ground endless. Dig deeper and find more back fill and red Conway Twitty records. Rain kept coming and the earth heaved an infinite stash of brick so that even an area that seemed clear of rubble would be filled again in a week's time, quickly enough to break a neighbor's spirit or force him deeper into the ancient, personal struggle against the land. As Jesse's crew worked others came to join them—and the hard impervious ground absorbed the newcomers as well. The *Star*, a community paper, published photographs to record the progress. That made the Liberty Lands real.

Marita Fitzpatrick showed up then, new to the Northern Liberties, missing South Philadelphia and the unquestioningly assertive bazaar. It was not the land that absorbed her. She was most attracted to the people and the community that had formed in the struggle— though as the weeks went by she found herself committed to the single seductive idea of transforming the lot into something beautiful and green. Even then, in the park's first year, work spilled into happy hour and gossip spilled into miniature soap operas and she discovered the richness in the local social networks. The park was functioning like a town square well before any visible progress had been made.

Marita grew up deep in South Philly in a model neighborhood from the early twentieth century called Girard Estates. It was built from the beginning around a square and contained all kinds of progressive notions about the urban fabric. Her parents sent her to a private school in the suburbs where the other children asked her how many families were living in her house. She understood then the disdain for cities among the first generation to flee. Blindly she took the sweeping, caustic, and bitter feeling, but she could never accept it. Marita wanted to grow things in the battered ground. She began to feel like she was part of something righteous.

It was not long until Marita was assisting Dennis in conducting the meetings of the park committee. The committee was formed to oversee and plan the work, but especially to elicit input and response from all members of the community. Dennis moved the group ahead slowly and carefully, ensuring that at each decision-making step a diverse spectrum of people had weighed in. The plan itself, which Jesse designed, appealed purposefully to a range of interests. It included a community garden, a playing field, a large gathering space, a children's garden, a wildlife habitat, and a butterfly garden. A group formed for each, which meant that Liberty Lands was really a collection of smaller projects. Leadership, then, was by process, and design was decentralized and open to many rather than a few. But Dennis, whose long freckled arms are spotted with gold paint, would not have wanted it any other way. He claims now that his interest was always solely in the mural that he designed and painted at the southern end of the park. Otherwise, he credited the success of the effort to serendipity and his initial instinct to stand by the project as others attempted to claim that a park would attract drug users and the homeless. And the word *interim*. A motion still stands in the official ruminations of the Northern Liberties Neighbors Association that says the park is just a temporary placeholder.

Nothing they planted at first would grow. The land would not even absorb water, only sweat and constant attention. Implementing the grant, responding to the paperwork, administering and upholding its requirements caused fearfulness, frustration, and tears. The gray, sullen earth took the tears too. Midway through the first work season—as the *Star* reported that lawyers representing a developer were meeting with the local councilman—the project seemed to have expanded beyond anyone's capacity to control it. Tessa, Dennis Haugh's first child, was born.

Perhaps then the scope of the endeavor was becoming clear. What had started as a unique, community-building vision for the Northern Liberties was now an extraordinary monster. Here was a band of neighbors, perhaps one hundred in total, who were attempting, on their own backs, in their own time more than anything else, to construct a community center from a two-acre patch, a slice of urban land worn thin by time and miasmal floods, made heavy by the weight of the land's history, collapsed and inert in their own muddy hands. What a terrifying spectacle! And there, the municipal authorities stood astride waiting to judge them worthy or not. Would the half-a-million-dollar distending weight of the lien placed on the property (to equal the cost of the buildings' demolition) be removed in honor of this effort or would they have to toil longer and lobby City Hall harder and plant more and dig faster and shorten the range of their own internal dissension? Would it ultimately crush the effort?

The questions hung over the project for years, always in the front of the minds of the leaders of Liberty Lands. And the questions came to symbolize a larger question about the roles and responsibilities of people and their government to provide public services and public gathering spaces, the role of government in planning the city. Who should toss the seed of the city's change? To this, Jesse Gardner said, over and over again, as the park took shape, as ripe and teeming green came from hebetudinous gray, *We can build it!*

Spring wore on to summer. The evening air became thicker and hotter and the white, ample, and sugary pear tree blossoms dropped to the sidewalks below. Green leaves replaced them and violas planted months earlier in the silent hope of new warmth now sulked, brown and chaste. The work became harder as the hot air throttled the neighbors' strength and the sun was no longer kind, but cruel and cursed. But they continued working the soil, coaxing life. They placed wood chips down to decrease acidity, black gold, made from the previous autumn's leaf collections, in the garden plots, and Earthlite, really sewage sludge given to them by the water department, everywhere else. To spread the Earthlite, they rigged a medieval contraption, six feet long, constructed from rolled turkey wire fence and a log. Like peasants in a muddy Slovenian field, but without mules, they heaved rope pulleys that rolled the log that dragged the wire fence, like a rake across the land.

Jesse Gardner, the only one being paid on the job, with an out-sider's naïveté and openheartedness, sought labor from every corner of the neighborhood. Not always at first but eventually, he found the work crew becoming more diverse. With little sense of decorum and a New Yorker's bright and assuming face, he coerced free equipment and donations from vendors. He organized additional volunteers into teams, teaching skills and holding everyone to professional standards.

On a spring weekend Jesse hand built a retaining wall from stone collected from the site. The wall came to symbolize for him the entirety of the park itself, of city building, of people coming together with a shared goal and learning from each other. Wall building is one of the ancient skills, like carriage making, like making a living as a wheelwright, that cling to Jesse Gardner as the city clings to its inhabitants. Like parasites, the skills survive through him. Jesse is by nature a teacher, so the skills are passed along a little further. When it was completed, the low wall looked like it belonged hidden in a field of larkspur and aster. But there it was on American Street behind the roses.

The rose bushes were not originally to stand in front of the stone wall. They were planted in the early shallow soil along Third Street, to measure the street in red blooms. Before the next morning had come, though, a dozen were gone, and another dozen the night after. They moved the bushes and they moved on.

In time, Jesse became the pied piper of the project. He relied on Dennis to mediate continued board opposition to the park and on the association's president, Rita Fitzgerald, to master the paperwork and cut the checks as necessary. The photographs of school children with shovels and neighborhood residents with wheelbarrows and Jesse with blueprints continued to make the project real and lasting. In the public's mind, to the African Americans and the Latinos and the Ukrainians and the Polish, to the musicians and the artists and the free spirits and the libertarians, the park existed. The large trees were proof, the sweat and exhaustion proof, the stone wall proof, the garden plots proof, the railroad ties proof, the arbor proof, the stone and brick piers proof, the talk and happy hours, and the new social networks proof. After no more than ninety days of struggle, Liberty Lands had become something beyond a pulsing vision. It existed real as the eyes could see it, ugly and awkward like a newborn and rocky, the soil now brick red and weedy, altogether more like an abandoned field in the backyard of someone's gray house in Booneville, Mississippi, than a park in the nation's fifth largest city.

The demolition lien was still not settled and would not be through the second work spring, or the third. Rumors about developers continued to make the leaders of Liberty Lands nervous. The fear was milder now. Time and burnout and fatigue had caused so much lassitude, as if they wouldn't mind if their blood would have flowed in vain. But in the third summer, Dennis's mural stood bright against the sky. He had painted the creek and the mill. He attached enormous wooden bees and a sultry orange butterfly, purple coneflowers, and trumpet vines, shell peas and hand-built birdhouses. The earth itself was now green at least in patches. Neighbors came to watch lawn-chair cinema. For the second year, Liberty Lands was part of the city's ten-day July Fourth celebration. There on the park's particular day of the festival, the mayor waved the lien.

Jesse Gardner, who had been hired to be a taskmaster, who knew only to look ahead each day and pound like a blunt instrument on barren ground, whose weekends for two years were spent not in some quotidian relaxation but instead racing back and forth like a buffalo across an open field—or at times more like a beheaded chicken beating circles around a pen or a rocky field of yarrow—found himself contending now with a baleful of love from the neighborhood. Fearless and confident, he gives the love back. Now he rejoices in the park on Saturdays, gardening his own plot with his wife, helping neighbors plant street trees on another block. It is not unusual for Jesse to feel tears spilling as he works. He has moved to the Northern Liberties of course, to a house not a block from the park, and he can go there any day he chooses. Jesse is a volunteer now, one of the crew. But can he savor the rare and hesitant pause?

Marita Fitzpatrick's pale green eyes are intense. Each day she walks north and west out of the Northern Liberties to a school named for the poet Paul Laurence Dunbar, where she teaches art. She returns from school, walking through Yorktown, the heralded neighborhood of African American stability, past the mayor's house, and back to the Northern Liberties. Marita now oversees the community garden section of Liberty Lands. It keeps its own rules and constitution, and she manages the turnover of the plots. There among the first volunteers, she is a new leader of Liberty Lands. With the brutal struggle over, she is faced with limitless ambiguity. Perhaps she feels as the ancient Jews did once they had finished rebuilding the temple. What now? Nothing left to do but pray that the seed they cast will take root. But prayer is not enough to sustain a city.

The neighborhood association has formed an open space committee with the idea of creating a miniature, local park system with Liberty Lands as its centerpiece. Already volunteers from Liberty Lands have begun to plant trees and work on other small corner gardens. But leadership is contracting. Most of the park's volunteers now are school students from the neighboring Bodine High School for International Studies who have constructed an international garden and those who maintain individual garden plots. Marita has noticed a new sense of entitlement, neighbors demanding a garden plot in return for their volunteer time. She misses the constant sociability of the previous years, though all that networking has resulted in a new association of neighborhood artists and endless hours drinking Will Reed's choice beer at the Standard Tap.

The sign inside Liberty Lands is nailed to a wood post: *This is Liberty Lands Park. This park was created by neighborhood volunteers.* They created the park and they own it. They set the rules. They take responsibility for what happens here. They manage and care for the place. But minus the enormous task of building it in the first place, the take-back-the-power approach has begun to falter.

In the fourth spring of Liberty Lands, neighbors constructed a playground in front of Dennis's mural and a soil irrigation system was installed on the common. But everyday maintenance is uncertain. Sod is sometimes planted where it should not be. Work is repeated needlessly. The herb garden languishes. With one fire hydrant as the central water source, it is nearly impossible to keep new trees wet enough. No one believes the park is pristine. The ground itself is rocky and uneven. Brick and concrete pieces crowd the surface and a surly openness dominates, like a vast and unshorn meadow.

But calmness prevails over this community-owned park. The municipal government is no longer lurking in the shadows, nor are developers, and neighborhood leadership is focused on the redevelopment of the nearby Schmidt's brewery. City officials have always been passive in the process of creating the park. City Hall took the first hit by paying for the demolition of the tannery and then by writing off the cost. Without that effort, none of the rest would have been possible. It is nowadays the way the City of Philadelphia operates, without planning or foresight. It is reactive. The buildings were dangerous so down they came and then, what? The neighbors stepped in, assembled resources, made something of trash. The city waved the lien, but it might not have. The neighbors made an astounding leap of faith given the almost savage disconnect between the government and its people.

Still, the city remains passive. It surely doesn't want another park in its already underfunded system, and the neighbors will be hard-pressed to ever give up control. But how long can the neighbors' association sustain the park? Where does municipal responsibility start; where does it end? How much can a group that represents a neighborhood of four thousand people but without authority to tax, accomplish without the day-to-day assistance of a larger body, and on the backs, by and large, of volunteers?

Marita faces these questions on a rainy Saturday morning in a café a block from the park. She has just come from planting spinach, lettuce, and nasturtium. She gave another gardener a forsythia bush; she is addicted to the garden. Often she sees others in Liberty Lands, others from outside the neighborhood, who have walked by or who have taken their Saturday lunch on one of the benches. Marita tells them the story of the park, the proud story of neighbors coming together behind a vision, of working and sacrificing, and of this tangible result, a gift to everyone. It is a familiar story in the Northern Liberties. Ask them how it feels to have saved a patch of ground, and they respond how wonderful it is to have made these new friends, how fortunate they were able to come together at the right time, in the right place. Jesse describes the love he feels for the neighborhood and Dennis the momentary serendipity and Marita the beauty in the garden. Not one of them feels like a hero. Not one is ready to face hard questions about management of the park. It is still too soon.

We spread seed across the city blindly. We take four years, as the builders of Liberty Lands have done, and give every moment to the future. We work as if in a trance, in the euphoria of city building. Dennis, Jesse, and Marita—and hundreds of others—built a new city park in the Northern Liberties. From someone else's ash, they crafted public space. It was a momentary explosion of joint energy. In their hands, their soil, and their trees, the city survives. The

Liberty Lands is a gift to everyone and to generations to come. They hand us a new city. We accept it, but for how long?

Imagine a group of people who toil for years to build a park without any guarantee that the park will stand even through their own lifetime. After all, the Liberty Lands is officially a placeholder. We might call them crazy. Yet they have done what all of us do with the city—absorb and reinterpret it, then pass it along. All of us capitulate this process. We give our lives to the city. The city demands it. It has no other way to survive.

What we build, though, only lasts so long. Tessa is three now, tall and thin like her father, and she sneaks crab apples from the ground but doesn't smile much. Her shoes are red like her hair and she rides up high on Dennis's shoulders. On the ground below her, purple-black violas crest the gray light and a row of lilac shocks the air preposterously sweet amidst low phlox and wind-blown pale yellow daffodil. There is milkweed growing and a butterfly bush, sedum, yarrow, a Shasta daisy, bee balm, and mint. Each plant is light and hopefully green. But Dennis feels sanguine and tired. He finds no perfection here, no miracle. He keeps no plot in the community garden but one behind his old-fashioned town house on Fifth Street. The Liberty Lands to Dennis, its creator, is hardly a jewel. As if to prove his apparent melancholy, he notices that one or two of the handmade wooden bees that are attached to the mural, the bees he had dreamed of to symbolize the old Bank of the Northern Liberties, whose motto was *never at rest*, busy as a bee, busy as the relentless volunteers who attacked this project, are missing wings. He wonders when they will grow them again.

16. PERCHANCE TO DREAM

MY friends and I spend a lot of time imagining the city. *If there were a Fifth Street subway. . . .* It always starts out like this. *If there were a Fifth Street subway, in ten minutes I could be eating empanadas in a Dominican café. Not just Fifth Street, we need four more subway lines—and a canal on South Street.* And a square to replace the parking on the Headhouse. And a pedestrian bridge over the Schuylkill at Locust. *Hey! I'd just like to see a law banning chain-link fences!*

Our Philadelphia allows us to dream. The experts tell us that the city's fifty-year population decline is the perfect opportunity to reduce the city's density, to build at a smaller scale. *People don't want to live so close to their neighbors*, they say. To our informal planning commission, the population and industrial decline is the perfect opportunity to amass land for large, inventive, multiuse real estate projects. Spending other people's imaginary money, we think big. Having seen some of Europe's most creative new projects—that often incorporate high-density residential development with retail, open space, and transit—we dream of the possibilities for Philadelphia.

The fact is we all do this. Every citizen in every city in America has ideas about their physical, intellectual, and cultural environment. Our dreams are the seeds of tomorrow's cities. All of us—the neighborhood activist who fights for safer streets, the children who brave gunshots to play in an open field, the policymakers who introduces immigrant-friendly legislation, the group of artists that develops a school of painting—indeed all the people I interviewed for this book—have the opportunity to plant those seeds and watch them grow. But planting the seeds—and raising the plants—can be difficult and frustrating business. That's why some of us stick to our dreams.

What? You don't hear it? Listen now, here it comes. Listen to the voice of the announcer. *Fifth Street train making stops: Independence Hall, the Liberty Bell, el bloque de oro.* Empanadas anyone?